MW00677812

Just Chasing the Sun

A unique collection of short stories and poems

Dixie Ann Black

www.Dixieannblack.com

DIXIE ANN BLACK

Enterprises

Tallahassee, FL

Dixie Ann Black Enterprises
Tallahassee, FL
(850) 556-6983

Visit our website at: www.DixieAnnBlack.com

Email us at: DixieAnnBlack@gmail.com

Cover picture by: Dixie Ann Black

Cover Design by: Diane Bass Designs

ISBN: 9780692399262

LCCN: 2015903830

First printing, March 2014, USA
Second printing, March 2015, USA

TABLE OF CONTENTS
Introduction

Introduction

I made a bold claim when I called *Just Chasing the Sun* unique. Here is what I mean.

This book is a personal journey on many levels. It is a reflection of my thoughts and feelings as I traveled the world seeking out its treasures, and as I sat in my own home searching for the treasures Within.

The format of the book adds to its uniqueness. Each story is followed by five poems. The poems initially relate to the story but expand in scope. In the same way the stories are at first personal, non-fictional accounts (names have been changed to protect privacy), then move to fictional stories.

The book starts with a nonfictional account of a safari my friend and I took on our trip to Cape Town, South Africa and ends with a fictional story about a young man on his own journey in Cape Town.

The title poem, *Just Chasing the Sun,* is also about a journey. This poem is found in the last section of the book as we (you and I) journey back to Africa, symbolizing our journey around the earth. This and many other poems such as *Holy Vessels, Ebb & Flow* and *Love Will Not Fail* were Spiritual gifts. They came to me complete and without the struggles of editing. They reflect some of the things we learn along the path of affirming who we already are when we are our best selves. Our quest for affirmation in the world is summed up in these lines from the poem,

I chased after God and ran after love

But all I was doing was chasing the sun.

Some have suggested I change "sun," to "Son." I leave that to you to embrace the One that is life for you.

My prayer is that *Just Chasing the Sun* will be life to you. I trust that it will delight you and bless you in a deep and abiding way.

One Love,

Dixie Ann Black

dixieannblack@gmail.com

Fairy Glen, Cape Town

Fairy Glen Safari

Fifteen of us climbed up into the military style tractor as our ranger guide began his introductions.

"Keep your arms and legs inside the vehicle and DO NOT stand up unless I instruct you to do so. There is an 80 percent chance we will be charged by a Rhino, an elephant can tip the vehicle and a lion will climb it."

Sitting in the very front I had an intimate view of the handsome face that delivered the ominous news. But it was the indemnity clause, releasing the tour company from liability that flashed across my mind. I had signed it casually and quickly, without a sense of danger. Now I wondered if this dark, swarthy man with his charming accent and "GQ" good looks would be the last thing I'd see. "God's got jokes," I thought.

The ranger refused to carry a weapon, saying it made him look incompetent. Now, let's see; incompetent or dead? I can live with a little incompetence, I thought. But he was not privy to my thoughts, so we moved on.

As we headed into the bush, I looked more closely at the only thing that stood between me and death. I had climbed up quickly (and excitedly) into the tractor. I had been more concerned about being on time and getting a good seat than about what the vehicle meant to my safety. The diabolical ranger yelled out, "Seatbelts everyone!" then chuckled as he observed our confused efforts, then added as a deliberate afterthought, "Oh, that's right, there are none!" The vehicle was an old farm engine with iron bars to grab on to in front of each row of seats. It had a wide metal frame which provided support for the tarpaulin that shaded us from the sun. There were no doors or bars to keep us in or to keep the animals out. The noise of the engine was so loud one had the feeling you were riding in a large lawnmower.

The noise left me of two minds. *The animals could hear us coming from miles away and may hide,* I thought. *We would surely be scaring them off. Or, we could be frightening them and they might attack.* Since it was too loud for conversation, I wrestled with my dilemma until the sudden lurching motions of the vehicle captured my attention.

"Here are the creatures I detest," the ranger was saying. He had been attacked and hospitalized for nine days due to injuries sustained from a male ostrich. His broken ribs, punctured lung and various wounds from the bird's beak had healed. It was obvious from the aggressive lunges he made with the vehicle toward the birds that he had not forgiven the beasts. Nonetheless, his professionalism prevailed and he provided us with fascinating information. "An ostrich's brain is the size of a pea. Its egg is equal to about twenty-four chicken eggs. The egg is able to withstand over 120 kilograms

9

of pressure. All parts of the ostrich can be used and its meat is the healthiest to eat, making ostrich farming a very lucrative business. All birds have vocal chords and make a noise except for the female ostrich. Why can't that be a woman?" the ranger asked. I suddenly understood why the ostrich had stomped on his head.

The terrain changed to a softly undulating plain backed by the majestic Brandwacht Mountains. Soft white clouds completed the picturesque scene and various species of antelopes gracefully bounded out of our path. The Springbok, South Africa's national animal, was by far the most distinctive of the gazelles.

"The Springbok can go for two years without water," the ranger was saying. They are able to survive without water by seeking out flowers, seeds, leaves and shrubs before dawn when they are most succulent. These beautiful animals displayed in shades of brown with white underbellies that keep them cool in the hot South African sun. They presented a beautiful contrast as they pranced by the wildebeest. But we were on safari, seeking out the Big Five: the lion, the leopard, the elephant, the rhinoceros and the South African Buffalo. We were reminded that since the leopard was nocturnal, it was unlikely that we would encounter him on our day trip.

We headed to the lion's domain on the preserve. There were three adults, a male and two females, who had been segregated from the three young lions. Dennis, our guide, justified the fencing and security gates around the mature lions as follows, "If the elephant escapes you say, 'There goes an elephant.' If the lion escapes..." His voice trailed off, leaving our heightened imaginations to complete the scene of carnage. There was a collective shudder among the group. We let the summer sun warm and reassure us that this was only a thought. In this atmosphere, we crossed a series of security gates and entered the king's domain. Dennis warned us that the lions were in estrous. A male lion in heat did not welcome intrusion. Luckily, he was preoccupied when we approached. Lions

10

mate every few minutes but each coupling lasts for about fifteen seconds, we were told. These large cats live about as long as a house cat, roughly fifteen years. Their roar can be heard for miles. We approached perilously close. The lions looked at us with lazy gazes and walked by neither threatening nor threatened. They had other things on their minds. "A lion has about a twenty percent success ratio in a hunt. Because of this, they never know exactly where their next meal will come from. This makes them opportunistic hunters. They are prone to attack unpredictably." (A comforting thought for someone sitting on an exposed old lawnmower.)

Next, we sought out the rhinoceros. The male, a massive five-thousand pound beast, had attacked several vehicles in the last few weeks. He had impaled the side of our vehicle on the previous tour. He eyed us with suspicion as the noisy vehicle approached him. Dennis parked at a seemingly safe distance. The female grazed quietly, obviously unconcerned, but the male began to position himself as if he felt a threat was imminent. I wondered briefly why my normally level-headed friend, Lyn, and I had opted to put ourselves in harms' way.

In this age of technology, we could easily download stunning pictures of this massive hunk of armor and view a STILL close-up; all without the need for an indemnity clause. The guide was explaining that the rhino's horn was made of creatine – the same protein found in the hair. It builds muscle and acts as an aphrodisiac. Over 300 rhinos had been killed last year for their horns. I looked at the massive bulk several yards away. This one would not go quietly. Our disquiet had been assuaged by the guide who pointed out that the huge hunk of danger had very poor eyesight. As long as we stayed still, we had the advantage of being able to escape before he figured out where we were and tried to gore us. I looked again at the majestic mountains and let the awesome view ground me. THIS is why we are here. I took heart and the guide moved us away from the belligerent animal.

We rattled along over the unplowed parts of the reserve in search of the elephants. When we found them, the 15,000 pound friends were playing in a gravel pit. "Elephants carry their young in utero for twenty-two months, so why do women complain about nine months?" Dennis quipped. The elephants displayed a surprising amount of personality. Dennis informed us that they often walked "home" in the evening with their trunks tossed carelessly over their tusks as if it was too much trouble to carry the additional weight so late in the day.

The zebras kept their distance. The giraffes loped along unconcerned by our presence but my favorite animal, by far, was the little donkey. He was on the reserve when the rhino had gored and killed the hippo a few weeks earlier. He probably witnessed the hippo's kamikaze charge. He may even have had a clue why the hippo had decided to attack the belligerent beast. Little donkey had been donated as food for the lions. But, like the fairy tale characters, he was too skinny. While he was being fattened up, he won the hearts of his keepers. He was unlike every other creature on the reserve. Nonetheless, the little black burro mixed and mingled with all the beasts. He was plump and happy. To the observant eye, it could be noted that he stayed close to the edges under the trees. I preferred to think it was because he preferred the company of the antelopes and zebras to the territorial rhino.

Regardless of his reason, little burro was safe from the sacrificial alter of the butcher or the teeth of the lions. He took his chances daily with nature as is every creature's right. I was happy for him.

Our last brush with death was our close up visit with the South African buffalo, the meanest creature on the reserve. Mean and ugly. Our rustic military lawnmower was moving in closer than anyone on board felt was wise. Even our reckless ranger seemed to be proceeding with caution. He was saying, "… make no mistake, he will kill you. He has a demon in him. This is not an American water buffalo. He can NOT be domesticated."

As we approached, the huge black male stood, peed and began his approach to our vehicle. Dennis had stopped the vehicle and was seated on the front rail with his legs dangling over the edge. The buffalo started to snort and we started to sweat. My friend, Lyn, ever the diplomat, said quietly but clearly, "I wouldn't be upset if you decide to leave now." Not known for tact, I added a little too quickly, "If he charges, you will fall out and I will drive this thing out of here." He ignored me, caught up in the folly of male bravado.

The other thirteen people in the vehicle began to squirm audibly. The buffalo came so close we could count the bumps on the mantle across his head. He snorted and pawed in what every rational creature instinctively recognized as a warning. Dennis rattled off some facts but I didn't hear them. Being trampled and gored by a South African buffalo was not how I envisioned ending this incredible trip to Cape Town, South Africa. "If you run, he will chase you." Dennis was reading my mind. After an interminable wait, he started the engine and we were on our way back to the lodge. The buffalo followed slowly, his vengeful glare piercing us from behind.

The rustic spacious lodge had an expansive lunch waiting. The amazing presence of the incredible animals took back seat to muscles in cream sauce, seafood paella, steamed cabbage and more... all against the back drop of granite and Sandstone Mountains and verdant valleys.

A local Cape Townian targeted my friend and me with unsolicited commentary. "Your source is here," he said. He peered into our eyes to see if we understood. "Your roots are in this soil. You have come home. The Cradle of Humankind is located close by and the two peoples dispersed from it, the Khoi and the San." He rattled on like an encyclopedia.

The majesty of Africa was tapping me on the shoulders again. His voice was echoing in my heart, "You have come home."

The Path Home

Womb of Creation
Your pain has not been in vain.
From the dawn of time you have labored,
Your riches have birthed the beauty of civilization.

Cradle of Humanity
Forgive the woundings of errant children.
We had to leave to find our way.
It is the only path back to ourselves.

Mother of Mankind
Our loss calls us back
To the root of our soul,
Your sons and daughters will find our way.

Wealth of a thousand nations,
In you is our verdant beauty.
The plant is nothing without the Soil
Africa, your children will come home.

∞

Awakening

I start to hear
The birds' songs in the trees
I start to see
The beauty that surrounds me
I start to be.

∞

The You I Seek

I sat in the empty café by the sea
Looking with every incoming wave for your love
I looked until my neck ached and my heart broke with longing.
Then a gentle wind turned my vision away from the sea
And into the long forgotten depths of me.
And there I found you
Shining like an orb of persistent light.
*You **are** the ocean living inside me!*

∞

My Rhythm

You are the part of me
I searched for and could not find,
On the shores of time.
You are my rhythm,
The reason for my rhyme.

∞

Holy Vessels

The devil called a meeting of the demons
He had charged with the job
Of tormenting Christians and stealing their earthly joys.
He started off with hate and malice,
The job they'd done was puny and wrong.
One by one they reported, then were booed off with a gong.
The crowd grew timid as it thinned,
No one had made the mark;
That's when Ignorance stood up to talk.

He was bolder than the others, he even giggled with glee
Then to Satan he offered this report as a final plea:
"I've got them where you want them, Boss,
You have no need to worry here.
The greatest ministers and evangelists
All have to bow to me.
They sit and fellowship and eat
And this is when I take my seat.
I pass the butter and the salt in large amounts
Like major treats.

Then when this part is over, I simply pass the sweets.
There's hardly one that can resist an apple pie or potato chips.
Their arteries have so much sugar and fat they all could make their
very own dips.
They eat anything in a box as long as I put the word 'Food' on it.
Then they hurt and ache and cry and ask Heaven
'Why, Oh Why?'
He sends them to the Book,
But even there I have them hooked;
They're so busy working on a pure and holy mind,
They leave their bodies way behind.

17

Just Chasing the Sun

They like to suffer with their aches, they think,
It a good Christian makes!
And when they're really desperate
I give them some pills to take.
They don't know a vegetable
Unless it's caked with salt or grease.

As for fruit and water, they yell
'Pass the sugar please!'
Then comes, cancer, diabetes, old age and heart disease.
So with this blissful ignorance
My job's really quite a breeze."

Then he sat down with confidence looking quite at ease.
Satan's smile was slow and cunning, he called two more Demons,
Then he sneered,
"You need help for the time is drawing near,
If we can't tear them from their God, then let's add some
Doubt and Fear!

Let them accept the food we give,
Never even questioning, let them pray, that's okay.
There're many more meals in each day!"

∞

My Grandfather's Funeral

"Here you go. Thank you." The heavy set American tourist smiled at the tall, slender luggage attendant as she handed him a ten dollar tip.

"That's okay. You have a good time in Jamaica." He quickly handed the ten dollars back to her and walked away.

The woman turned toward the waiting JUTA tour bus, stunned and embarrassed. She stepped on board the bus wondering out loud what she had done wrong. Earlier her friend had advised her against tipping, but she had felt compelled to give something. She had painstakingly fumbled with the exchange rate between the Jamaican and United States currencies before coming up with her offer. Now what? Her first experience coming off the airplane had quickly turned sour.

The other passengers on the bus wondered out loud with her. Why had the attendant refused ten dollars? After a few minutes of discussion, they turned to the only passenger on the bus who had said nothing.

"Do you know why?"

"You gave him ten dollars in Jamaican money; that is less than twenty-five cents in American dollars." I said quietly.

"Oooh." The woman groaned as she determined that she had actually insulted the man.

"You didn't know. And he knows you didn't know." I added. She didn't hear me. She accepted her shame like a cloak and covered herself in resignation to her embarrassment.

"Do you know how long this ride is?" The couple was on their way to Ocho Rios. They were to be married on Sunday. The delayed flights had brought us to the island late Friday night.

The normally spectacular view of the ocean and mountains was now shrouded in darkness. The journey between Montego Bay and Ocho Rios was under construction. The normally bumpy road literally vibrated with gravel and potholes. It had been over a half an hour since we set out and the hungry couple was starting to wonder if they would get a meal tonight. When told the ride would take another two hours they swallowed hard. The older man in the front passenger seat of the tour bus appeared to experience the most trauma from the driving experience.

Apart from finding the vehicle riding on the left side of the road, he had had the questionable pleasure of watching oncoming traffic heading straight at him in their attempt to avoid potholes. He chattered nervously as he watched the driver switch to whatever side of the road was free; or run off the road unto the sidewalk in order to give way to overtaking vehicles. All this while careening into the darkness with no street lights to warn of approaching dangers. The constant shaking and turning of the vehicle over the rough winding roads finally led him to announce that his hemorrhoids were all gone.

Nearing Ocho Rios two hours after leaving Montego Bay Airport, I stepped off the bus with a reminder to the tourists to buy from local vendors and try the Jamaican beef patties and Red Stripe Beer. My father picked me up from the nearby gas station a few minutes later. We headed directly to my grandfather's home.

I heard the booming music long before we parked the car and took the rocky 300 yard climb up the dark path to the house. "What's going on?" I asked. There was a live band playing reggae music surrounded by a crowd of young people. We passed them and climbed the two sets of stairs to the verandah. Here the older folks sat overlooking the darkened ocean and listening to the commotion below. "It's a new thing," my Aunt Vee explained.

Instead of the traditional wake known as "nine night" where family and close friends sat around, talked, sang and danced to folk songs, the local funeral homes had begun a mutation.

20

They now provided all night bands. The singers took turns drinking strong black coffee and salt to keep their bodies and voices going until seven in the morning.

They sang a free mixture of reggae, reggae-style gospel and folk songs. This attracted every partygoer and freeloader in the community. The family struggled to keep the food, soft drinks, ice and alcohol going all night.

"Useless" made himself useful by running drinks and food back and forth all night. I finally summoned the nerve to ask if I were understanding his name correctly. Yes, but... Having been born with a disability his own mother had nicknamed him "Useless."

No one remembered his real name. Someone surmised that it was "Ulysses" or something remotely resembling the current mutation. Ironically, despite his severe speech impediment, this man made himself extremely useful. When I suggested that he be renamed "Useful" they told me the rest of the story.

Apparently "Mr. U" (a man in his forties) would visit the homes of those who had recently experienced a loss. He would do odd jobs and make himself very useful throughout the critical time immediately preceding the death. His only request in the way of payment was daily food. The problem came once the funeral was over. Mr. U would stay on indefinitely.

In fact, it was difficult to get him to leave long after his "usefulness" had ended. He usually had to be forcefully evicted from a property. With this history, it was unlikely that he would experience a name change. This in no way bothered Mr. U. He was at home in his place in the community. The community in turn accepted him as one of their many anomalies and thus his position was preserved. And for now, he stayed in the spotlight as almost everyone called on him for more of ice, curried goat, rum punch and more.

At 2:00 a.m., I announced for the third or fourth time, "This is madness. I want to go to bed." My father reluctantly walked me down the hill and drove me to our cousin's house. I gratefully sank into the comfortable bed and prepared for dreamland. Fat chance. The windows throughout the house were open, letting in the gentle, cool Caribbean trade winds…. and the noise (music) from the family home a mile away. Exhaustion finally won, I fell into dreamless sleep.

"If you want to go with me to Port Maria, you have to come now." Daddy awakened me abruptly with this statement. It was 8:00 a.m. He had not been to bed but exuded the energy of a man revitalized by his surroundings.

He headed for the car, insisting that I did not have time for a shower. Defying him I jumped into the shower. The shock of the ice cold water brought me fully awake. Now I knew I was home. Our family never had a hot water heater during my childhood in Jamaica. Returning home always meant adjusting to cold showers.

The ride to Port Maria about thirty miles away was everything I remembered and longed for. This port town is located in the lush parish of St. Mary on the north coast of the island. The blue green sea sparkled on the left for most of the drive. On the right, verdantly lush trees, multiple flowering plants and mountain ranges interspersed with colorful buildings lined the way. Seemingly unending varieties of bougainvillea, hibiscus, ginger lilies and orchids stood out from every nook and cranny where soil could be found. Banana and coconut palms along with mango, breadfruit and ackee trees held promises of delicious meals within reach.

Mizerah Funeral Home held few of the buffers offered by American parlors. My father and I walked into a garage like area and were directed toward a small room. The door was already ajar and we could see the cadavers lying like lifeless mannequins on wide tables. We were told to identify my grandfather's body. Stepping deeper into the 8x10 room, we looked over the six dead bodies.

One, of a middle aged man lay by itself. (I fleetingly wondered what had ended his life so abruptly.) An older couple lay on another table. (Had they even known each other in life?) There was no time to contemplate what were now irrelevant issues. The third table held a young man and two older men. One of which was my grandfather. The bodies were all completely nude. It appeared that the practice was to take all the bodies scheduled for burial that day and lay them together in a room for identification and dressing.

My grandfather (known to his community as Uncle Mack) looked very much the way I remembered him when I saw him the year before, except he now had a moustache which had grown since his death. Daddy verbally identified the body and handed the attendant the suit he had brought for the funeral. The attendant looked it over quickly and added slyly, "He needs underwear and powder." Daddy said he had not been given these instructions by my aunts who had made the preliminary arrangements.

The attendant was ready with his reply, "I can get those for you for $500."

"Five-hundred dollars?! Why does he even need underwear and powder? He's dead! Who will know he's not wearing any?" My mind hadn't made the conversion to U.S. currency right away. I tried to whisper to my father that I strongly suspected that the $500 would end up in this man's pocket and we would be none the wiser. Daddy, compelled by the dignity of the situation and the 3:00 p.m. funeral deadline, quietly paid the additional fee.

The drive back to Steer Town was a quiet one. Both my father and I were engrossed in our thoughts as the island sunshine wrapped us in its healing warmth.

A brief stop in the famous resort city of Ocho Rios allowed us to pick up the wreaths and a quick lunch of local fruits and breads.

Back at the family home, we dove into the confusing family dynamics of who was doing what job and who would drive whom to the church. The hearse would be arriving at the church around 2:00 p.m. and we were left to find our own way there to receive the casket and begin the final viewing.

The Methodist church was a beautiful new structure located at the crest of yet another hill overlooking the ocean. The inside of the building was well-lit with natural light provided by large open windows and a high ceiling. The floor was tiled with large lightly colored tiles. New wooden benches lined the walk up to the raised platform at the front. The casket was placed at the top of the steps in front of the entrance of the church. Without air conditioning, the balmy afternoon breezes were not trusted to preserve the body for very long.

I watched my father. Earlier he had handled identifying the nude cadaver, buying $500 underwear and paying hundreds of thousands of Jamaican dollars to the funeral home, all without flinching. Now he glanced at the dressed body in the open casket, bit his lip and turned away. An old friend close to him, apparently unaware of his grief, chattered away. Or maybe he, too, was shifting his grief. Daddy's voice broke and I was moved to see him so moved. My three uncles and two aunts walked around the church in a daze, each one obviously precariously near tears.

This was the end of an era. Uncle Mack, "Papa," to his children, was the last elderly parent, the last grandparent for those in our thirties and forties. He was a gentle man in the true sense of the word. He never raised his voice, yet was firm. His sense of humor was legendary. His skills as a folklorist and musician were renown. He led the yearly musical parade known as John Canoe throughout the surrounding towns each Christmas. Memories of him sitting on his veranda in his special chair, overlooking the ocean, blowing on his harmonica filled the minds of all who knew him.

The church was filled, although most of the "partiers" from the night before were missing. Somehow I suspected many of them would show up again at the home after the funeral for the final meal.

The family sat close together in the first two rows. Everyone held their own, quietly containing their emotions until my Aunt Trish let out the first holler. Here we go, I thought. But I was wrong. Daddy transferred his grief into comforting her. Others shed quiet tears or quelled them with stony silence. The traditional wailing and gnashing of teeth so typical at our funerals never came. Tributes were spoken, read and sang. I was asked to speak since Papa's children and the grandchildren who lived in his household up to the time of his death, did not trust themselves to speak without breaking down in front of an audience.

The light breezes grew still with the somber weight of grief. The sadness was eventually replaced by boredom as the minister took center stage, droning on and on and on…He was no longer speaking of Uncle Mack but seemed to be relating all of his most loved Bible passages to a captive audience. I began to wonder if Uncle Mack was indeed wearing those $500 underwear. I wondered if anyone would have the nerve to check. I had not been able to detect even a hint of powder.

Relief came (to me, at least) in the occasional yells and vehicular sounds of passersby on the road outside…and in the incredible view of the sea visible from the pews through the huge open windows.

At the graveside, the daughters (my aunts) huddled, comforted by their sons. The sons (my uncles) hung back. The choir sang, the minister read, the daughters cried. Uncle Mack (Papa) had lived a long and full life. He was eighty-seven years old when he died. His quiet strength had effectively communicated his unconditional love for his children and grandchildren. He had passed on a strong work ethic as well. His children had memories of him going fishing or farming in the predawn hours of the morn. He would always return with something with which he could feed his family. Now, in a small community where many were out of work, all of Papa's children earned a decent living. Leaving the cemetery, or graveyard, as it is most often called in Jamaica, we let ourselves be bathed and held in the warm sunshine and intoxicating beauty of our surroundings. All but two of Papa's seven children and several of his grandchildren lived in the United States. Returning to Jamaica was like stepping into healing springs for us. The stresses of American life began to peel away with every day we spent on the island. Lulled by the gentle lapping Caribbean blue and the sing-song voices of our people; we were re-energized by the passionate warmth of the sun interspersed with playful breezes.

We piled into cars and headed down one hill to the family home. Daddy pointed out places where he had played cricket as a youngster. He recalled out loud the friends and the mentor he had as we wound our way down. It was as if with the intensity of the funeral events behind him, his heart and mind could now expand to take it all in – past and present. We climbed the next hill on foot as we returned to the home. It was time to reflect with close friends and enjoy the afternoon meal. As the family settled on the veranda my father walked up and without any apparent thought, sat easily in the chair formerly reserved for my grandfather. He looked out unto the sparkling sapphire blue of the Caribbean Sea and I was aware that with the ending of an era, a new patriarch had been crowned. The future had begun.

Ocho Rios, Jamaica

For The Dollars of Strangers

Gone; the innocence of your lowlands,
Replaced by houses built by Others
Where you trade your treasures;
For the dollars of strangers.

Gone; the beauty of your beaches.
Jet skis, cruise ships and cheap tricks,
Not for your children;
For the dollars of strangers.

Bare; your splendid hills and mountain peaks
Trees and treasures traded for gaudy pleasures.
Secret places sold for a necklace of concrete
along your once pristine coast.

Outside those gates of presumptuous luxury
Your children roam barefoot and hungry for hope.
Jamaica, Jamaica, that I know and love
Are you gone forever?
Paying the price for progress in this material world
Do you live on only in my nostalgia?
Or will I again see the beauty
Of the land of wood and water
Land that I love?

∞

Silhouette

If I could paint a picture of love
It would be the clouds kissed by the sun
The shore caressed by the ocean
The trees yearning for the sky
The sands yielding to my feet
And the silhouette of lovers
Basking in the beauty of it all.

∞

Vapor

Contentment is an elusive vapor
Hidden in the pain and complexity of life
Gratitude is a bitter flavor
An acquired taste not easily savored;
And peace, the Holy Grail,
Is the distillate of a life at war;
The deep darkness which births the dawn.

∞

Pretty Wife Snacking

Her beauty
No longer self-sufficient
She feeds on the dainties of desire
And slowly the shadow of her discontent grows
Eclipsing her peace
Stealing her joy
Unearthing anxieties
That outer arms cannot soothe.

∞

Goodbye to Southern Spring

I will miss the dogwood blossoms
Dancing mysteriously in the dark
The wisteria bringing life
To long forgotten vines.
And the azaleas,
Littering every nook and cranny

∞

Corner Piece

Toronto, Canada, is famous for the CN tower, St. Lawrence Market, the Toronto International Film Festival and a host of other attractions but none of these are how "The Big Smoke" first captivated me. For me, it provided the setting for finding a major puzzle piece in my mother's life.

I believe we are born holding the pieces of the self we are destined to be. Life then conspires to shake the pieces from our grasp. The full canvas of our lives spills like pieces of a puzzle even as we begin to reach for who we are. We spend our lives searching, and if we are willing to look beyond the obvious for who we are and where we belong, we find the pieces in often unexpected places and reconnect them to find ourselves.

On Memorial Day weekend 2012, my mother and I took a trip down nostalgia's dirt roads in search of one such puzzle piece. The fullness of who we are exists beyond the present and the future; it is deeply rooted in our past. We flew from Florida to Canada and found that the past is as close as the next bend. That journey was a three hour airplane ride, but for all intents and purposes, we had taken a trip back to Jamaica in the 1960s.

Weeks before, I had watched my mother transform before my very eyes. Mom had foregone travel in favor of work for decades but suddenly two tickets were purchased for Toronto, Canada; mine and hers. Having learned that there would be a reunion in Canada of her childhood friends, she had immediately committed to attending it, insisting I travel with her to meet her old friends. She had moved Heaven and Earth to locate old acquaintances living in Toronto. Nina and Jack were just as excited to hear from her after five decades. They insisted we stay at their home for the reunion.

Suitcases and clothing choices littered her home for days and when we boarded the airplane, most people assumed she was my sister. This attractive woman in her late sixties took on the affect of a stunning younger woman.

The city of Toronto reminded me of the cleaner, gentler America I envisioned existing in the 1950s. Nina and Jack picked us up from the airport and gave us a quick car tour through downtown. They lived two hours outside the city and with its population of over 2.5 million people, they did not miss its hectic pace. As we rode Nina informed me Toronto is called the Big Smoke due to pollution. But today the air was clear and crisp. We would have stopped to tour the CN tower and look up close at other city sites but mom was anxious to get to the house. As her self-appointed chaperone, I felt obligated to defer to her wishes.

My mother was literally beaming with excitement and anticipation. Her eyes sparkled as she readily jumped into every conversation that began with, "Remember …?" There was, "Remember when…" and "Remember Mr. So and So.." or " Ms. So and So… …" Listening to the old friends, I had the image of a large box of puzzle pieces being dumped in front of them for assemblage. They approached it with gusto and soon the pieces were taking on images of the past, crisp and clearly represented in the present by their effort to connect them.

I tried to analyze the essence of the difference I saw in my mother. She is generally a positive, energetic woman but this new found vibrancy had a rarified quality. Connectivity? Belonging? Hope? She had lived the last twenty-five years in a land disconnected from her roots. Now those roots sprouted new tendrils in eager anticipation of renewed connections.

The reason for the entire trip was summed up in one thought, 'reunion.' For the past six years, the Racecourse Reunion was held in Toronto, Ontario. This weekend long event offered various opportunities to reconnect and was highlighted by a formal dinner/dance called 'The Ball.'

The Ball was held from Saturday evening into the wee hours of the next morning then followed by an afternoon barbeque on Sunday. It encompassed several generations of students who had attended the Racecourse school. Connecting these activities were streams of memories that were rehashed over kitchen tables, telephones lines and on car rides. For the Jamaican Diaspora born and raised in Jamaica but living in countries all over the world, this and other reunions like it are major events that feed the almost palpable yearning for the beauty, life and culture lost due to migration.

Most of the attendees had kept in touch with a nucleus of the group. Attending the reunion always meant reaffirming bonds and finding yet another piece of their past in some long lost student who had made their way into the present. Despite all differences, the commonality each shared was a strong and clear connection to the common ethos of Jamaican life; education. Schooling was the bedrock of the Jamaican psyche and in this group, everyone had stories of abuses suffered at the hands of the now infamous Racecourse teachers. Some attendees had gone on to earn doctorates, run their own businesses and achieve other marks of success. But here, everyone was proud of only one thing, their association with Racecourse school. It was more than a school, it represented a village. Some were reaching back and helping the students who lived on the brink of hope in the small community. In fact, the organizers of The Ball, were veteran supporters of their old school. Proceeds from the weekend's event would go toward the education of the children back home.

Returning to the village over fifty years later, my mother found again her childhood, neatly placed in Toronto, Ontario. The fact that her first childhood took place in Racecourse-Clarendon, Jamaica and she has been living in Florida for over twenty-five years, has only added to the spiritual nature of this tale.

"Remember the people who used to sell food at the school gate? They would sell Drops and Gizzada," Nina's pretty eyes were dancing as she spoke.

"Niece used to say I would eat from a sore foot man!" The outrageous insult to a woman so fastidious about hygiene summed up the abuses my mother suffered at the hands of this woman. I looked closely and found my mother's eyes glazed over by the past, the flush of emotions connecting it vividly with the present. She and Nina had not seen each other in over fifty years. They continued reminiscing with gusto.

"...And patties and fritters," Nina added. You could smell the foods as if she spoke them into existence. Her husband Jack flowed in and out of the conversation like a familiar vagrant. He added post mortem insight into the psyches of the abusive adults from their past that still loomed larger than life. The beatings were now worn as badges of honor.

"Remember the belt Teacher Handsell use to beat us with?" Mom had the unusual distinction of never having received a beating. Her father was wealthy and respected in the area. She was the only child who was driven to school. Everyone else walked.

The privileged life she was born into came to a violent and abrupt end. At sixteen, my mother was chased out of her family home and her community by the squatter who had assumed the position of wicked stepmother in their home. 'Niece,' as she was called, had arrived ten years before on the heels of her departing mother. The beatings from her husband had proved too much for my grandmother. So with a promise to return for her daughters, my grandmother had shooed her crying six-year-old child back home and disappeared down the lane with only a small suitcase.

Her other two children were four and almost two-years-old. They didn't understand what they were losing, but even at six my mother knew, and it broke her heart....broke it so badly it took the next sixty-two years to find most of the pieces.

So mom had not grown up with her village in the usual sense. It had been lost to her since the day her mother left. In its place was an emptiness that nothing had filled. Mom migrated to America in the nineteen eighties, losing her community for the second time.

Here we were at one of the major confluences of that great oneness called time. Mom had left her life behind at sixteen. In those days, leaving a community was like leaving the planet. With no cell phones, no Internet and not even readily available transportation or telephone systems in those days, she had lost her entire past. Through the years, she had often reminisced about what happened to the people she had the most in common with. Born to a more cynical time, I had often encouraged her to move on and make do with the blessings of the American life we had adopted. But mom longed for her past.

Then one day, she received a call from an old classmate who found her through a friend who had mentioned her to another friend, who happened to have her number...Mom jumped on the Internet and plunged into the social network to find what she had been searching for, for over fifty years. The Ball had a website and a Facebook page. The connections were reignited like dry kindling in the Florida heat. They blazed a trail of anticipation that ushered us into gowns, heeled slippers and brilliant smiles.

That Saturday night, the ballroom in Toronto was packed with over 300 people, all filled with zest for life, eating, dancing and telling jokes, each person proudly holding a piece of their puzzle in the spirit of unity. Each was the hero or heroine of their own remembered destiny. The connections of the past validated the full canvas of their memories as more than just fairytales. Like the awakening of Sleeping Beauty and the revelation of Cinderella's glass slipper, each person held a piece that said, "This is who I am!" But when my mother walked into the ballroom that night, both Sleeping Beauty and Cinderella curtsied and stepped aside with the realization that this was Mom's night to shine.

As she met and hugged old friends, acquaintances, teachers and various people from her past, the amorphous nature of each act congealed into one of those corner pieces that are essential for the completion of a puzzle. Mom had retrieved a part of herself.

Jamaican Rum Cake

Mother

Unbroken cord to my past and future
Womb of my beginning
Reflection of my past
Living legacy of bygone eras
Linking history to me.

Mother, tender truths of love's release
Cradling dreams beyond logic's harsh light.
Amazing love, birthing true humanity.
At once facing Heaven and Hell
Boldly demanding all, to give to me.

Bounties of love large or small
Squandered for love's tender call
Her eyes the pools from which I came
Her love, the reason for my fame.

∞

Still…

Taking form we alight
Unto this human plane
Of sight and sound and touch.
In every gesture
Between every thought
We reach for what was lost
Still sensing it is still here
When we are finally still.

∞

Fallen Leaf

A golden leaf traveled on a gentle wind to me,
Stopping before me to dance and glint in the warmth of the sun.
It wanted me to notice its beauty.
Below the clear water of the pond, tiny fishes darted to and fro
With a purpose I could not discern,
Seeming not to notice those above.
The leaf was dead.
But in death had turned a golden brown
Which when lit by the sun and carried by the wind
Brought life to me.

∞

Sunday Morning

The sweetness of Sunday morning
Still lingers in the air
A tender dew upon the grass.
The war drums of "Must," "Have to,"
The myriad stresses of daily life
Echo in the distance
Staid and held at bay for now
By the beauty and sweetness
Of Sunday morning.

∞

Ebb & Flow

The breezes blow because life is an ebb and flow
There is faithfulness in ebb and flow
There is faithfulness in abundance and in lack.

Spring's flowers and summer's heat
Are not cheated by autumn's winds or winter's cold.

Your gain is not the reason for my lack.

One day is not 'good' while another is 'bad'
Good and bad are judgments born of fear.

There is one Good and in Him all is renewed to goodness.

The rut of 'good and bad' stalls the ebb and flow of life.

Some become stuck on the 'good,' others fear the 'bad'
What if we lost the fear and embraced it all as Good?

Bad would be swallowed up in good.

Bad would cease to be.

Doesn't autumn's wind make room for new leaves?
Doesn't winter's cold give rest for the resurrection of spring?
Doesn't lack leave room for the joy of abundance?

When the breezes blow it is good, when all is still it is good.

When spring's flowers and summer's heat are replaced by
autumn's winds and winter's cold, goodness is all we behold.

Your gain is good and so is my lack.

Just Chasing the Sun

At the core of ebb and flow is goodness.

And at the root of 'good' and 'bad' is faithfulness.

So, faith in the goodness of God in all things;
Ebb or flow;
good or bad,
abundance or lack,
must mean only one thing:
It is ALL good.

Grasp this and we are ready to Live!

Free from fear of ebb or flow - FREE!

Free from fear of good or bad - Free!

Free from fear of abundance or lack!

Free to be faithful
To the One who shows Himself faithful
...in ALL things.
∞

Through My Eyes

Sighing with pleasure, I embrace the vibrant energy of my own body. I stretch from head to toe, enjoying the sensation of every fiber of my being. I wiggle my fingers and toes and float, suspended above my bed. This is my time. In the predawn light I can do anything, be anyone. Predawn is my magic moment. I rest here, letting the joy of *Being* envelope me. It is my morning ritual, my pre-waking rite before the sunlight dispels all fantasy.

All too soon it's six in the morning and the madness has started. Candy is working this morning. She is disorganized and none too kind. She bursts into my room and floods it with harsh electric light. My light fixture's shade broke some time ago and no one has replaced it. The bulb dangles on the electric cord over my bed and its glare is the first thing that hits me each morning.

She grabs me with a stream of words that are meant more for her than me. Swearing, she strips me of the sodden diaper. The bed is soaked and the smell of urine rises like a cloud that envelopes us. She grumbles that there is no time for a bath, since she has two others to get ready before the van arrives. She moves me this way and that, stripping off soaked clothing and putting on the first thing she grabs from the basket beside my bed. The ketchup stain completely escapes her attention. She doesn't notice the smell of sweat in the armpits of the shirt, nor does she realize that this shirt belongs to Chris in the room beside mine.

Three bowls of instant strawberry flavored oatmeal are sitting on the table when each of us is wheeled into the kitchen. Candy feeds Jamie first, he loves oatmeal. When she gets to me, the oatmeal is cold. I hate cold food. I hate strawberries. So I turn my head away. The sudden flash of lights on the windowpane tells us the van is here. We are rushed out, one by one and hoisted by a creaking lift into the sea of bodies already strapped in place. The smell of soap, sweat, food and urine form a disgruntled cloud in the air around us. But for now, at least the van is quiet. The day program is five miles away. I watch as we drive through the early dawn making intermittent stops for the next hour and a half.

Shirley's smile greets me and I am happy she is working today. I smile back and she lovingly coos over me and wipes dried oatmeal from the corner of my mouth. She wheels my chair into the large room with bright yellow walls and boxes all around. Other people are coming in and the sounds of wheelchairs, walkers and unsteady feet builds like the approach of a swarm of bees. It is exercise time.

The new girl, still filled with enthusiasm, puts on the Michael Jackson CD and turns it up above the din. She arranges us in a circle and encourages each of us to raise an arm, move a head or a leg. I stretch out my left arm. Encouraged by my attempt she grabs my arm and pulls it even farther. I cry out. She looks confused and a little scared. She quickly moves on to the next person. I scream louder as the pain mushrooms in my shoulder.

Derrick tells her I am always uncooperative during physical exercise and they move me into the music room. My shoulder pain is now a dull ache so I stop crying.

"See?" Derrick tells the music teacher, "He likes music, he doesn't like exercise."

Their perception defines my reality so I am subject to the clanging and banging noises being made by the others who can use their limbs.

I love my wheelchair dance time. Shirley teaches it. She helps me spin my chair around and she touches me often. Her hands are kind and firm and so are her eyes. I see something in them that makes me smile.

"Why are you wearing a dirty shirt?" She asks. She clicks her tongue in disapproval and takes me to the changing room. She cleans me thoroughly and then says, "I have a surprise for you!"

She pulls out a new T-shirt and asks if I like it. My eyes light up so she laughs and puts it on me. All the while, she tells me about her weekend. She bought the shirt for me at the flea market while shopping for her children.

When she is finished, she positions me in front of the small mirror and tells me how nice I look. I look at my new shirt with creases from the package and I look at Shirley beside me. Her shirt is old and torn. There is a dark bruise on her cheekbone just under her eye. I start to cry. She clicks her tongue in that way of hers and tells me not to worry, everything will be fine. She doesn't understand that I am crying for her.

Art is my favorite activity. Once the brush is placed in my hand and the paper is within reach the classroom disappears and I am again in that space where the predawn magic dwells. Each stroke reveals the emotions of my being. I speak with the circles and swirls and the hard downward marks of my brush. When they offer me colors, I paint the messages of my dreams. I could paint all day but soon my shoulder starts to ache from the effort. I stop and stare at my creation, the poetry of my soul.

"What did you make today?" The art teacher understands the beauty of imperfection. She sees the subtle differences in each of my pieces. She knows that I have spoken my heart. She hangs it to dry. "I think this one is my favorite, I like the way you mixed the blues and grays," she tells me. I will take it home and it, too, will be placed in the drawer beside my bed like countless others. But for now, I share the joy of creating with a kindred spirit.

All too soon the day is over and I am back on the van heading home. I look at the trees rushing by and wonder what they feel like. I wonder if the grass is as soft as my bed. How is it that the bird can fly and the dog is hugged more often than me? I do not see John lurch out of his seat behind me. I only feel the pain of his grip as he sinks his teeth into my left arm. I am screaming before I even understand what is happening.

The van erupts in noise and confusion. The driver slams on the brakes and John is propelled forward into the back of another wheelchair. Blood is everywhere. My arm is black, swollen and bleeding. John's face is bloody. I am not sure if it's from biting me or from being slammed into the chair. I don't understand what is happening. My world is clouded with pain.

The emergency room is a sea of helpless cattle. The walkers and talkers pace and complain but it does no good. Here they are like me, a task that intrudes on the hurried flow of other duties. The nurse yells her questions loudly into my ear. She subscribes to the common perception; *"Those who cannot speak are retarded and, therefore, hard of hearing."* I turn my head away. The doctor arrives, looks at her and crisply asks what happened.

"He was in a fight with another one of them. He hit the other one in the face so the other one bit him." The doctor nods curtly and prescribes something "to calm him down." He leaves the room without ever looking at me.

I awaken from the fog slowly. There is no floating or predawn light today. I feel wretchedly ill. Sam operates the house in which I live. He is standing beside the bed arguing with the nurse.

"Did you not read his admission packet??!! He has allergies! Did you not read his list of medications and precautions before you gave him the drug??!!" Sam was so angry I could see the veins on his neck. But the nurse was calm and cold.

"The doctor prescribed the medication. You have to take that up with him." She turns and walks out of the room. Sam walks over to me and leans in to speak. He stops in mid thought and swears. He rings the bell for assistance and a cold voice across the intercom asks what is needed. Sam demands to know the last time I was changed. He is informed that that would have been the responsibility of the overnight shift. The nurses' aide was currently busy and I would have to wait my turn.

Sam yells into the intercom that I have been there since the previous afternoon. The intercom is silent. The voice is long gone. Sam swallows his impotent fury and searches the room for fresh supplies.

I am home again. My week in the hospital has left me weak and drawn. I am several pounds lighter and I have a cough, but I am home. My bare room with its broken lampshade and basket of soiled clothing feels like an old sweater. Sam cleans up my room and yells at the staff about the mess. Soon he will be leaving to work at his other job. But before he goes, he gives me a shower and sits with me.

We have a history deeper than time. He has been my helper and friend since the day we met in the house of many halls. He tells me old stories from our past and plays checkers with me. He watches my eyes to see where to move my piece. He never cheats so he never wins.

Finally, he sighs and gently pats my left arm. "They've cut our funding again, but don't worry…..." he looks away. He promises to see me soon. I know this means his visits will be fewer and farther apart.

When I awaken, I expect the sterile nurses and the noise of many instruments. But this is Saturday and I am home. At first I am confused, Sam is standing over me. His smile is as big as his heart. It melts away the groggy stupor of medications and I smile back.

He doesn't explain why he is there but his movements are quick and he is filled with excitement as he gets me ready for the day. He picks out my best shirts and has me choose one. Then with an air of suspense he asks, "Are you ready?" He can't seem to contain himself. He does not wait for a reply. He wheels me out of the room and down the hall, then into the living room. There is a strange stillness before the world explodes.

"SURPRISE!!!" The disembodied voices emerge from the corners and take on familiar shapes. There's Chris and Jamie, Derrick and Shirley, among the host of faces. They are all smiling at me.

On Sam's cue, they burst into song, "Happy Birthday to you...Happy Birthday to you..."

That's when I notice the balloons floating on silver strings like the moon through my window at night. The giant cake with white icing is surrounded by a mountain of freshly grilled hamburgers on the kitchen table and beside me the half broken side table is laden with gifts wrapped in every color in the rainbow.

Sam leans down and whispers in my ear, "You didn't really think I'd forget your birthday, did you?"

There is clapping, shouting and laughter. I am hugged and squeezed and spun around in my chair until I am dizzy. I smile so much my mouth hurts.

Sam unwraps each present and puts each one within my grasp. Today my choices for breakfast are oatmeal, or hamburgers, cake and ice cream. My smile widens and Shirley takes the cue.

She brings me a plate with hamburgers, chips, cake and ice cream and the biggest bottle of Root beer I've ever seen. "Now you know you have to eat something healthy...tomorrow."

Someone puts on a Michael Jackson CD. Shirley and I dance. As is our custom, Sam guides each guest to my chair and I dance with each one. The day is a blur of color and light, music and laughter.

It is late when Sam helps me into bed and when I close my eyes to wait for morning I find that I am already suspended in the magic of the predawn light.

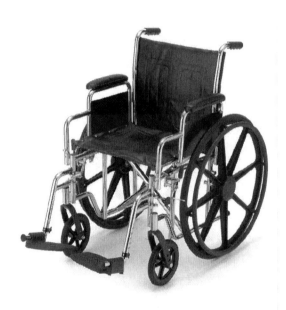

Be Still and Know...

She spends hours staring into space
She is oblivious of time.
She speaks the truth in childlike verse
She is oblivious of lies.

She reaches out for kind hands and a smiling face
She knows the touch of love and grace.
She takes time to love
She has the time to care.

She moves slowly on limbs not fully formed.
She cannot be hurried, stress is not part of her world.
She is dependent on you for her care.
She is trusting, she has no fear.

Her smiles hold no reason, her thoughts no rhyme.
She is free from the confines of space and time.
She is still...and she knows...
What will take you and me
A lifetime to learn.

∞

Outcast

There once was a man who didn't have a hand
His eyes had lost their lashes.
He stared night and day in a most awful way
At his warts and his rashes.

The children he scared had not ever dared
To approach him for fear they might catch it.

Yet he smiled at one and all
And even tried to call to anyone who would listen.
But since he had no teeth and was forced to eat
Things that squished and would glisten
No one was brave enough to come close to this knave
For fear they might then be missing.

Yet one little lass ignored the bad gas
And the puss that oozed from his toes.
She came close to him with his toothless grin
And he told her all his woes.

She listened kindly and stared blindly
At the sores upon his nose
And for once in his life
Despite peril and strife
This man had found a friend.

∞

Domestic Violation

Who will weep for the children?
Daddy is chained to his childhood
Mama is held by her past.

One stands, shoulders stooped
A broken slave on the auction block;
His manhood for sale.

The other's been made into the master's whore;
Working with little hope for more.

History endlessly repeating
In new scenes of human desperation

And the children cry,
For the parents have forgotten
How or why.

∞

Teach the Children

O my people listen well
I will teach you the secrets of life
I will give to you the treasures of our fathers.

O my children listen well
And I will teach you what to say
And you my children will teach someone else someday.

My secrets are the wonders of the Lord
He has done mighty deeds and is worthy of praise.
He has given us laws of life and covenant love
For all our days.

O my people listen well
And teach the ones not yet born.
Teach them to obey the Lord
Let truth and faith be planted deep.
Teach them to remember His deeds
And to give thanks with tender hearts.

Then our ways will be blessed
And our inheritance secure.
Teach the children of the Lord
For in His knowledge they are strong.
(Based on Psalm 78)

∞

Project Health Blues

She fries bacon in the nude
It reflects her shameless attitude
Pain is the seasoning on the dish life served
No sense in screaming she won't be heard.

Labeled by her choices and by society
She lives in dark places housed by poverty
Like an animal that's left on its own
She survives hardship and makes it her crown
Everything has a price and she barters with the best
Even though in school she flunked every test.

A loaf of bread for a pack of cigarettes
Trading life for death with no regrets.

Everything's for sale she's too poor to own
All she has is borrowed, stolen or handed down
A welfare check and a disability paired
Her life is branded, labeled and seared.

She belongs to the throng that is faceless and poor
Too expensive to face, too many to ignore
Living on the crust of the American pie
Nobody will care if they live or die.

∞

51

The Darkened Door

Stacy specialized in finding customers the perfect house. Dwayne needed a house, urgently. The two had never met but their worlds were about to intersect in a realm of mystery and intrigue.

Dwayne had relocated to Florida three weeks earlier. His job had offered him the transfer but had not been generous with their offer. The moving stipend had been minimal. He was wasting money staying at the B-rated motel a couple of miles from his new office. After looking around at the rental prices, he realized he would be better off buying a little place right out the gates. He was that type of guy, decisive, practical, and logical. He never wasted time on inane details. He saved all of his attention for his work. So he called a well-known local Real Estate firm and was referred to Stacy. They arranged to meet at 6:30 the very next evening at the all night diner next to his motel. At 6:49, Dwayne sat at the table facing the door, tapping the table impatiently with his fountain pen.

He had arrived fifteen minutes early and was on his third cup of coffee. His already square jaw was set and his lips showed no hint of knowing how to smile. He adjusted his black square rimmed glasses as the door opened. His eyes were glued to the door but he could not have missed her if his back was turned and his eyes shut.

Stacy entered, disheveled and frantic like a late summer storm passing through a cornfield. The door slammed behind her, and as if on cue, the pile of papers she was holding in her hand went flying. She let out a shriek and a couple of expletives. A kind soul sitting near the door helped her gather her belongings. She took a breath and searched the diner for her prospect.

Dwayne held his breath as their eyes met, with a sense of impending doom he realized that she was heading straight for him. He groaned inwardly as she plopped her papers on his table and extended her hand. "Hi! I'm Stacy. You must be Deewayne." He didn't take her hand but she seemed not to notice. She sat down with a small flurry, knocking over his water glass and soaking his copy of Technology Today.

"Dwayne." He corrected as he brushed off her apology and tried to rescue his magazine. He wondered how quickly he could get rid of this disaster sitting in front of him.

"Well, Dwayne, I looked up all the houses in your price range, stayed up all night and I printed out the best ones!" She immediately started shuffling through the pile of papers she had recently retrieved from the restaurant floor.

Ever heard of technology? Dwayne wondered irately as he watched her fumble to put the papers back in some semblance of order. Instead he said as kindly as he could muster, "I thought you would bring a laptop and show them to me online."

"Well I like the personal touch. See? Here's a perfect house for you right here in my hands," she shoved a slightly soiled paper at him, "plus I can't use the blasted things anyway," she muttered. The paper

53

almost dropped in his coffee and he was forced to take it to avoid another disaster. He looked at the paper and to his surprise found the one story bungalow quite charming and within his price range. Stacy watched him closely and nodded knowingly. "Nice, isn't it?"

In fact, despite his desire to get away from the storm of disorganization seated across from him, he found himself interested in seeing three of the ten houses she presented. She had listened well and done her homework. Each property had the basic elements he'd mentioned over the phone; large master bedroom, storage space, backyard, within five miles of his job and all were within his price range. He had bought homes before, so he did a quick calculation in his head. He figured if he really liked one of these three enough to purchase it, he would not have a lot more contact with the Realtor.

If he did not like any of the three, he would quickly thank her and move on to another agency where he was sure to find a more suitable Realtor. They left the diner on her promise that she would set up the visits for Thursday afternoon. As it stood, he only had to tolerate her for one afternoon while he looked at three houses; *easy breezy* as his grandmother used to say. But he was wrong. Dead wrong.

He waited at the diner Thursday afternoon and for the ten extra minutes it took her to get there, he wondered why he had not just found another agent. As the thought jelled in his mind, she appeared in the doorway. He felt a curious mixture of disappointment and relief. She beckoned to him and he followed her out to her car. *Whatever happened to Realtors projecting an image of prosperity?* He wondered as he climbed into the 1985 Toyota 4Runner. The door creaked as he pulled it shut and his seatbelt was stiff and difficult to fasten.

The engine sputtered but engaged after the second try. *I wonder if this thing even has air bags*, he wondered to himself. *Well, at least it's clean*, he thought as she shifted into gear and darted into traffic.

The first house was in a congested little neighborhood within walking distance of his office. It was an attractive three bedroom, two-bath with gray vinyl siding trimmed in red brick. There was a one-car garage and a neatly trimmed backyard containing a baby swing and an inflated pool. The house was occupied by a young family who had outgrown it. They were anxious to sell before the birth of their fourth child.

"They're around the corner at the park." Stacy seemed to read his mind as they headed for the door. Just inside the door, Dwayne tripped over a toy and almost went sprawling. He regained his balance in time to lose it again as a small rodent like animal lunged at his ankles.

"What the…?!" To his own ears the scream he let out was much too high pitched to be his voice.

"Bad doggie! Back in your cage!" Stacy corralled the barking Chihuahua and shut the door quickly. "They told me he would be caged. He must have escaped. Are you all right?"

"Of course!" This time Dwayne's voice was several octaves below its norm. They negotiated their way around shoes, toy cars, a hamster cage and a high chair. Dwayne's neatly organized bachelor mind could not make sense of the clutter. They made their way to the first bedroom. The clutter belied the dainty pink and frills. There was a tiny bed covered with pink and green ruffles and every type of stuffed animals one could imagine.

Dwayne, having regained his composure, looked the room over critically, took in the dimensions and calculated the effort needed to transform it into a practical home office. He kicked a small doll out of his way in annoyance as he examined the size of the closet.

They moved on to the second room. For a moment, it appeared as if they had stepped into another dimension. This room was neatly organized and spotless. It was slightly bigger and contained a well-made bunk bed, a small desk with two chairs, a small computer and a lamp. The walls were covered with posters of wrestling personalities, rock stars and cars.

In the north corner of the room was an ornate stand three feet high made of polished oak. On top was a small wooden box inlayed with glass beads and small stones. It glowed an eerie green as if it contained radioactive materials. Dwayne had been eyeing the room dispassionately until he saw the box. He was riveted. He walked slowly towards it and as if in a trance, reached out to open it. "I wonder what that is." Stacy's voice jarred him back to reality.

"Let's go to the next house." He said abruptly.

"But we haven't even seen the master bedroom..."

"Let's go now!" His voice held an edge. Stacy scurried around him leading the way back to the front door. He took deep gulps of fresh air once they were outside in the quiet evening air. It was summer with its humid, long, well-lit evenings. Stacy gave him a long thoughtful look but he was oblivious. He was visibly shaken and took several minutes to compose himself.

The drive to the second property was not far but heavy afternoon traffic gave plenty of time for Stacy's relentless chatter. She had sensed he did not care for the house and needled him until he offered her the obvious objections. The neighborhood seemed more suited for families with young children, it was too congested, and the rooms were too small. She relented and embarked on another round of inquiry.

"So, you just moved to the area, what brings you to our quaint little town, are you married?" She fired the trifecta of questions while managing to give him a penetrating stare as they inched along behind the evening escapees from the state office buildings.

"No, I'm not married. I'm too busy for anything that frivolous. I'm here because of a job transfer. I wanted a quiet place to concentrate on my work. I work for an innovation and design company. We specialize in research to bring new technologies to the market." Dwayne loved talking about his work and would have kept going if Stacy hadn't interjected.

"But what about your family and friends? I mean you're like mid-thirties, right? That's about the time most men start thinking of settling down." She gave him another one of her piercing glances. "Not me. My grandmother is dead and I don't have time for friends."

Stacy's look was quizzical as if she wanted some explanation for the strange answer. But she instinctively changed tack. "I noticed you freaked out when you saw that toy box in the room back there. What was that about?" She was not known for beating around the bush and her blunt approach threw him off balance.

"I had a box like that once." He swallowed hard as if the words had forced their way out without his permission. Then, he shut his mouth so hard and fast Stacy heard his teeth shut.

The second house was a yellow stucco two-bedroom cottage with a large den that could be used as an office. The traffic delay had ushered in the setting sun which bathed the house in a soft glow. The yard had seen better days. The shrubs needed pruning and vines had begun to creep onto the driveway.

"This is a foreclosure," Stacy explained as she watched his reaction. "It's been vacant for a few months." She unlocked the door and flipped the nearest light switch. Dwayne closed the door behind them and took in the scene around him with appreciation. An open floor plan allowed him to view the kitchen and living room area at a glance. Large black and white onyx tiles, black granite counter tops, white kitchen cabinets and black leather furniture against white walls with black and grey drapes made a pleasing study of contrasts.

The ceilings were high, trimmed with moldings and well lit with recessed lighting. This was the kind of house he'd sacrificed social and personal pleasures to own. His mother had often berated him for his withdrawal after his grandmother's death. But Nana was the one person who understood and accepted him. She'd indulged his every wish much to his mother's irritation. She had given him the magic box. It was magic indeed because he had been spellbound when she unveiled it at his seventh birthday party.

The other children had hovered around him as if he was a rock star. Nana had whispered in his ear that the box possessed powers beyond his wildest imagination and all he had to do was believe and his wish would be granted. And for a while it seemed he could do no wrong.

He lived in the magic of the box. But Nana got sick and no amount of wishing was enough to save her. When she died, all the magic went out of his world. He stopped believing and turned to science. There, he found comfort in facts and figures, formula and function. He didn't need people. They eventually died and if they were still around, they were busy judging everything he did.

Stacy's voice brought him back to the present. "Let's look around, but remember this is a foreclosure so there might be some unpleasant surprises." She spoke none too soon. They opened the door to the first bedroom and were knocked backward by the smell that assailed them. Old clothes, shoes, broken hangers, CDs, papers and various odd and ends were strewn all over the floor of the otherwise empty room.

Were they robbed? Someone must have left in a hurry, or maybe the house had been vandalized? Whatever the reason, Dwayne was sure there wasn't a good explanation for this mess. But that wasn't the source of the smell. Putting his hand over his nose he ventured tentatively further into the room. He stopped in mid stride as he saw the open door connecting the room to the bathroom. He could see the un-flushed commode. His stomach lurched as his mind grasped the reason for the smell. He backed up rapidly and gasped for air in the hallway.

"Like I was saying about foreclosures..." Stacy's voice trailed off as if no further explanation was necessary. Then she added, "But remember, all the problems so far are cosmetic so let's press on."

The door swung open easily as they entered the second bedroom where, thankfully, the air was stale but not nearly as foul. Stacy found the switch and immediately the room was flooded with light. To their amazement, the room was neatly arranged with a well-made bunk bed, a small desk with two chairs, a small computer and a lamp. The walls were covered with posters of wrestling personalities, rock stars and cars.

In the north corner of the room was an ornate stand three feet high made of polished oak. On top was a small wooden box inlayed with glass beads and small stones. It glowed an eerie green as if it contained radioactive materials. Beside the box was a small gilded frame with a black and white photograph of a silver haired woman wearing a black and white dress accented by an onyx and silver pendant on the end of a thin string of white pearls.

Dwayne walked slowly toward the table then stood in front of it. Stacy watched with curiosity. She held her breath, expecting him to open the box. Instead, Dwayne was staring transfixed at the photograph. She cautiously inched up behind him for a better look. She noticed that the woman in the photograph was cradling a small boy of about six or seven years. The boy wore black square rimmed glasses, had a square jaw line and bore a striking resemblance to Dwayne.

Dwayne's eyes hadn't moved from the picture as Stacy approached. "Is this some kind of joke?" he croaked in an angry whisper. Stacy was silent beside him and it wasn't clear if he was speaking to her. He reached for the picture. As his fingertips touched the gilded frame, the door to the room slammed shut and the room was plunged into utter darkness. "What the...?!" This time, Dwayne's voice held fear. For an interminable moment, they stood in the dark not sure what to do next. Then, Dwayne's ears detected the jangle of keys. There was a small click and with it a small bright light shone in the darkness. Stacy had located the small flashlight on her key chain.

"It is better to light a candle than curse the darkness." Stacy said as she led the way to the door.

She tried every light switch she could find as they made their way down the hallway but none of them worked. She opened the door to what must have been the master bedroom and offered to show him the contents using her flashlight but Dwayne declined. He made out the front door in the periphery of her light and headed for it. He stepped outside quickly not knowing or caring if Stacy was behind him.

When Stacy joined him in the fading light Dwayne was very angry. "What kind of stunt are you trying to pull?" he yelled. His fists were balled and the vein on the left side of his neck was visible. She looked at him calmly for a long time. When she spoke it was in a slow measured tone.

"Now just what are you accusing me of?"

"That was a picture of me and my grandmother in there! I owned a box like that one! My room looked exactly like that room. Like the last two rooms!!" He was beside himself as he blurted out the information. "How did you know? What are you trying to do?" His voice held an edge of cold calculation.

"That world doesn't exist anymore! It died when Nana died! Everything good died when Nana died." The ice in his voice broke as he spoke the last two words. She was moved with compassion as she watched the man before her become a seven-year-old grieving child. They stood in the quiet aftermath of his anger as the shadows grew and swirled around them.

"I am not doing anything but showing you the houses you chose. Now if you want to see the last one this evening, we'd better get going." Stacy's tone was suddenly crisp with decisiveness. She got in the car and started the engine.

Dwayne moved from impotent rage to petulance. "I don't want to see the next house. I don't know what you're up to or how you're doing it but I'm not playing along. Take me back to the diner. Now!"

Stacy said nothing as she pulled the car away from the curb. They drove in silence as the shadows thickened into a soft blackness. He did not know the way back to the diner but Dwayne began to feel more and more certain they were not heading for the diner. "Wait just a damn minute! I said take me back to the diner. I refuse to work with you. In fact, I'm going to report you to your supervisors!" He railed in fury.

Stacy was quiet. In fact, when the sound of his own voice dissipated he realized she was humming softly under her breath. *Jesus*! He thought. *She's psycho! I picked a psycho for a Realtor!* His mind started to scramble for an emergency plan. His orderly logical habits brought him back to himself.

He started to quietly analyze his situation. He was much bigger than her and she didn't seem to have a weapon. He had to go along with whatever her crazy plan was until he could get away or use his cell phone to call for help. But who would he call? He had no friends. If he called 9-1-1, what would he tell the police? Finally, she pulled over and stopped the car in front of a house. The porch light shone like a friendly beacon on the lonely street. She turned off the engine and just sat there silently.

"What's this?" But he knew it was the third house he had seen in the picture the day before.

"Since your grandmother died, you have abandoned your family, you have abandoned your life. It is time for you to put your grief behind you and find the beauty and magic of life again." She spoke with that same matter of fact tone she had used earlier. Gone was the flaky, disorganized air she presented earlier. She seemed to stare right through him in the gathering dusk.

"Who *are* you?"

"What do you know about my life?"

"Who put you up to this?"

"Go into this house and face your past." She took the keys out of the ignition and walked confidently toward the front door. Dwayne just sat there looking at her. "I'm NOT going inside! You must be crazy if you think I'm going to play along with your little scheme!" He shouted at her back. But Stacy did not respond. She simply unlocked the door of the house and walked inside.

I'll be darned if I'm going into that house, Dwayne thought to himself. But an hour later when Stacy had not emerged, his resolve was beginning to weaken. There were no other lights and he could not find his way back to a main road if his life depended on it. Yet, another hour later when the night animal sounds grew in the pitch blackness, his resolve had completely dissolved. The sounds grew closer, as did his fears. Eventually, fear of bodily harm outweighed his internal fears. He opened the creaky car door and walked tentatively up the driveway.

The house was a two-story Victorian styled cottage. In the soft glow of the porch light, the white trim of the window shutters stood out against the dark green exterior. The front door was slightly ajar as if waiting for him to enter. He could have sworn it swung wider in a slow arc as he neared. He stood for a long moment at the darkened door knowing intuitively that entering would change his life forever. He called for Stacy but knew she would not answer. There was much he had not told her. He had picked this house because it looked exactly like the one he lived in as a child. His grandmother had lived and died in that house, but it seemed many lifetimes ago.

The long suppressed memories surfaced slowly at first, like the first drops of a summer rain, then the flood of them swept him off his feet even as he stood there. The long summer nights on a porch just like this one with his grandmother sitting in her housecoat with a light shawl, knitting and entertaining him with stories from her rocking chair. She had enchanted him with stories of magic and fantasy. They lived in their own world. She called him Dee. It was the sweetest sound he'd ever heard. It was a secret name in the secret life they shared where all things were possible. He could be king or president, dancer or racecar driver, wrestling champion or wizard.

The magic box was where they stored their secrets and gained access to the other worlds.

As was their ritual, he would make a wish before opening the box. There were only two rules; whatever powers he assumed from the box must be kept secret and must be used for good. When he opened it, the entire room would glow with its green light and he knew he was transported to another place. He would be whomever he had wished and his Nana was always there; his ever faithful confidant, armor bearer, trusted helper. He realized now that there must have been a green neon LED bulb with a battery source hidden behind the fabric inside the box. There was no such thing as magic and there were no other worlds. If there had been magic, it would have saved his Nana when he came to it, pleading for her cure.

Now the need to enter the house became tangible. He realized the need had been there all along. Now it was illuminated as if by a streak of lightening in the darkness of his storm tossed soul. His subconscious motive became apparent to his rational mind. The demons of loss and regret haunted him. This is why he'd picked this house from the pile. He stepped through the darkened door with tears of sorrow and longing streaming down his face.

The house was shrouded in darkness but he did not need a light. He knew the layout like the back of his hand. He no longer questioned the lack of logic in his predicament. He was again a boy of seven retracing the steps of his wounded heart. He made his way directly to his old room. Like the previous two houses this room was an exact replica of his boyhood sanctuary. Without stopping to flip on the light, he walked quickly over to where the box should be. He was surefooted. After all, he had made the journey hundreds of times before. He stopped and with total confidence, reached for the box he could not see. The beads and stones of the box were cool to his touch. He caressed the outer surface for a long moment as thirty-year-old memories and heartbreak overflowed his heart's walls. He sobbed the desire of his heart as he had the night his Nana died. The night he stopped praying, stopped believing, stopped hoping, stopped living.

"Nana." He sobbed over and over again. When he could sob no more he lifted the lid of his magic box. The room was immediately bathed in a green glow and from the darkened door behind him came an unmistakable sound.

"Dee..." He whirled around almost knocking the box off its stand.

"Nana!"

"Yes Dee. It's me."

Before him stood a sturdy older woman with silver grey hair pinned in a bun at the back of her head. She wore a white flowing housecoat with tiny flowers embroidered on the collar and sleeves, fuzzy pink slippers and a green shawl. She wore the onyx and silver pendant that had never left her neck even in death. Dwayne rushed toward her, "Where have you been? Why didn't you come before Nana? Are you going to stay?" The questions tumbled over themselves like unruly puppies each trying to be the first one out the door.

"No Dee, I've moved on and so must you." He was standing right in front of her now. Her words brought another wave of sobs which broke the dam of his self-control.

"I've missed you so much, Nana. Every day of my life I've missed you. Nothing is the same. Nothing will ever be the same." His body was wracked with sobs and in his desperation, he reached for the ethereal figure with outstretched arms. For a split second, he felt nothing but air. Then the smell of talc, freshly baked cookies and mint that was his grandmother filled his being. And the arms that held him so securely as a boy, wrapped around him now in comfort. He placed his head on her shoulder and felt for the first time in thirty years the reassurance of his youth. For an indeterminable moment, they stood there defying time and form in the comfort of love's embrace.

"Dee, you stopped living when I died. I've moved on and so must you." She repeated the last sentence with increased emphasis.

"But Nana. There is no one else. I am alone." His voice assumed the bewildered tenor of his youth as he contemplated the truth of his own words. His parents had never had time for him and with the passing of his Nana, they had left him to tumble up with food and shelter but not much more. He was the last of six children in a family that could scarcely afford five. Plus, he was different. He was questioning and needy. His siblings had a camaraderie that excluded him. They resented him for stealing time from sports and dates when they were forced to babysit him. His youngest sibling was ten years older than him and his parents had often referred to him as their mistake. He had come along in the dawn of their twilight years. They had spent his youth scrambling to make it to retirement.

Nana's living with them had saved them on childcare costs and on the time they would have needed to put into raising him. When she died, they had promptly sent him off on a scholarship to boarding school where his fragile world of fantasy was the subject of ridicule by his peers. Education had been his ticket to a life free from his parents' mundane existence; science labs, his refuge from the taunts of his peers; money, his substitute for relationships.

"Being alone is a choice. You have to choose to open your heart to others, Dee." She interrupted his protests, "Dee, you have brothers and sisters. Your parents are getting along in years. It's time you forgave and made amends. It's time you found a wife." He opened his mouth to protest but again she silenced him. "Dee, everything happens for a reason, no matter how painful. Without your pain and isolation, you wouldn't be the man you are today. Without my death I wouldn't be free. It was time for me to move on. Now so must you." He had never given much thought to his grandmother's suffering during her last days. He'd never entertained the thought that death might be better than life or that his suffering should be embraced. He'd just smothered it and let it eat at his heart. He stood there with his head on her shoulder for a long time soaking up the healing comfort of a mother's love.

"Time to move on, but I'll be watching, Dee."

The streaks of early dawn streamed softly in the window as the words stirred Dwayne back to consciousness. He was embarrassed to find himself curled up and tucked into the bed on the bottom bunk. He stood up quickly, too quickly. His head hit the bar of the top bunk.

No longer a child, he thought. The revelation shocked him in its reach. The ghosts of his past had been laid to rest. He was ready to move on. He took a step toward the box and realized he was holding something in his hand. He opened his hand and found himself holding the onyx and silver pendant.

He searched the house but found no sign of Stacy. Outside her Toyota 4Runner was nowhere to be found. The neighborhood was coming alive with people heading out to work. He stopped a couple apparently on their way to work. No, they had not seen anyone or a vehicle outside.

"That house has been empty for years," they said.

He called a cab and returned to the diner. He called the Real Estate brokerage but they assured him they had no one by that name working for them. They were quick to offer the services of another agent. "Maybe later," Dwayne told them. He knew he would never look at Realtors the same again. Wherever Stacy was, he knew she would be showing someone the perfect house. But a house was no longer his first priority. He booked a flight and then called a number he had not dialed in years. When a frail voice answered on the other end he said, "Mom, tell Dad I'm coming home."

I See Your Fear

*I see your fear
(because it is my own)*

I see you hovering

*With arms too weak to reach out and grasp
(this weakness lives in me).*

*I see your glaring and your subtle faults
(there is not one that is not mine).*

*When this veil of life's current realities is removed
It will be seen clearly*

That we have walked and talked

And lived and died

As one.

∞

Left Alone

Left alone and incomplete
In the desert of Purity
Until my cells are parched
I gladly take draughts of
contaminated water
To live long enough
To hope enough
To be enough.

∞

The Destroyer Is Here

Even now the Destroyer is here
The iron teeth of death, disease, derangement
Bite into humanity like a ravenous lion
Devouring its prey.

Family strife, sexual perversion, selfishness, poverty
Hatred, greed, apathy, covers the people
Like a blanket of doom.

'Time is of the essence' while 'busyness'
steals 'time' from all that is sacred.
The illusion is complete.
The Anti-Christ has arrived.

∞

Lazarus Come Forth
(Jamaican Patois)

Y'all been sittin' on yo butts for too long man
Talking 'bout what de white man did to yu';
Who you used to be back in de day
In Africa, in Antigua, Jamaica
And God knows where else.

Yu' behind is in de past
Growing grass
Get off yu' rass!

Yu live here, Now.
Who you, now?
What you goin' do 'bout "Now"?
Turn 'round wife of Lot!
Get up Lazarus
And come forth!

Fine yu' dream
Get out of de slum o' complacency
And do somethin' 'bout NOW!
Not de same ole same ole
O' haughty words puffed up by inaction.

Put yu' han' to de plow Now
Do a new ting, Now
Stop de preach and start to reach
Fo' who yu' say yu' are
An' what yu' say yu' want to see
Do it, Now.

What Does it Matter If...

What does it matter if
Segregation and discrimination
Still exist,
When we can't reach for our brother's hand
To lift him up?

What does it matter if
There's a glass ceiling
And affirmative action is outlawed
When we can't look into each other's eyes
And embrace the belonging we find?

What does it matter if
The U.S. rules the world,
Oil is found in Alaska,
Israeli and Arabs sign… or fight…again
Or Christ is seen in the Golan Heights
Or Westland Mall,
If when we stretch our arms out wide
There's no one we enjoy being beside?

Black and White, Arab and Jew,
Rebel and Rule, Rich and Poor
Are only contrasts of a deeper divide
That keeps man from man,
You from you
Me from me
Deep down inside.

∞

Temple of Heaven: Forbidden City- Beijing, China

Serendipity Cafe

The Chinese have a saying, "He who has not been on the Great Wall is not a great man."

Alexandria may be a hair over five-foot and 105 pounds soaking wet but she's a greater "man" than most. Don't get it twisted, as she would say, she's all woman, but this little nineteen-year-old is all dynamite. I have no doubt that our rickshaw driver on the streets of Beijing would agree.

At 4:00 a.m. on a cool morning in May, we loaded up the car and started the two-and-a-half hour drive to the airport in Jacksonville. Alexandria took the wheel of the Toyota Avalon with quiet determination. It is not easy for a mother to trust her teenage daughter behind the wheel at seventy miles per hour but exhaustion got the better of me. She sped on and I drifted into a light doze. The explosion rocked the car. I instinctively grabbed the wheel to steady the car. It was not necessary. Alex was calm. She slowed to a stop on the side of the highway. We had blown a tire and did not have the tool to change it.

Roadside assistance took one-hour to arrive. Anxiety needled us as we watched the time seep away. Mosquitoes from nearby woods swarmed around us and we rolled up the windows trying to block out the more persistent gnats of our anxieties. It did not help that we had been stranded on this very strip of roadway years before. Florida panthers haunted these woods and the memory of huddling in the car with my two small children while dark eyes watched us came rushing back.

When the tow truck driver arrived, our hearts sank. His raggedy old truck seemed to be in a predicament of its' own. He searched with a lethargic air for a lug tool and we began to despair that we would ever see Asia. When we pulled back onto the road, we were forty-five minutes away from the airport and our flight was scheduled to leave in an hour.

Our two-hour departure window had been whittled down to fifteen minutes, if traffic was kind. This was the only connecting flight to Japan for the day. Missing it would mean foregoing the entire trip. We raced up to the ticket counter fifteen minutes before take-off. When TSA stopped Alexandria, we felt all was lost. But we made it on board. A two-hour layover in Chicago and we were soon traveling at 500 miles per hour at an altitude of 38,000 feet covering our 6,000 plus mile journey to Osaka.

In Tokyo, we again wondered if we would set foot on Japanese soil. As the airplane prepared to land, we were ordered to put on masks. The plane was boarded by airport agents who were suited up like astronauts. The Swine flu pandemic was spreading rapidly through

Asia and Japanese customs was making sure no one brought the virus into the country. They moved around the airplane with high-tech instruments taking readings of our body temperatures. It was like a scene out of a Sci-Fi movie.

It would have been simply a fascination if Alexandria had not developed a slight fever and began sneezing somewhere over the Pacific Ocean. My being a bit of a "germaphobe" came in handy for us. I dug into my purse and convinced her to take every packet of emergency cold medicine I could find. The fever retreated at the onslaught of vitamin C, zinc and Echinacea. The instruments could not detect fear, so we were allowed to step onto the soil and richness that is Asia.

When I suggested we visit Beijing after visiting her sister in Osaka the year before, Alexandria did not hesitate. She saved her money and paid for her own ticket from Florida to Narita, Japan. There, we didn't have to worry. Natasha spoke some Japanese, Alexandria was learning the language and Natasha's fiancé, Takeshi, is Japanese. Still, panic assailed Alexandria when she ran ahead into the elevator without prior instruction. As the door closed on her, we could hear her shouting, "What floor? There is no English! What button should I press?!"

Fortunately, Natasha came to her rescue. Cocooned by her knowledge and experience, we visited temples, restaurants and shopping areas effortlessly. Kyoto amazed us with its mixture of old and new. We marveled at the hills, shrines, temples and winding roads and exclusive geisha. It was Japan's capital for over 1,000 years until Tokyo claimed the title. With thousands of temples and shrines to choose from we packed in as much as a day could hold.

Ginkaku-ji Temple, also known as the Silver Pavilion, is not silver but an unpainted brown, reflecting the Japanese idea that plain can be beautiful. And it is beautiful indeed. The grounds flourish with amazing landscapes. Kinkaku-ji, the Golden Pavilion, is

74

breathtaking with its real gold leaf covering as it reflects in the water of the mirror pond surrounded by Zen gardens. Now a Zen temple, this historical site was also originally built as a retirement home for a shogun. The three-storied temple floats like a golden ornament nestled in the beauty of tranquility.

The view of the Kiyomizu-dera (Pure Water temple) is spectacular. It is comprised of twenty wooden buildings all built without a single nail. It is replete with legends such as wish granting waters and people jumping off the terrace as a sign of courage for good luck. There was an eighty-five percent survival rate. So I suppose simply surviving the fall was proof of good fortune.

We traveled by train to Japan's oldest capital, Nara. It was even more beautiful with its rustic scenes, sacred wild deer and monks wondering the streets. We toured various historic sites but our visit to the Todai-ji temple was the most memorable. The temple was first built in 730 A.D. and includes the world's largest wooden building, the Daibutsuden Hall. This, in turn, houses the world's largest bronze statue of the Buddha Vairocana. The seated Buddha reaches a height of forty-five feet. That may be memorable as an interesting fact but many visitors to the temple that day will remember it for another reason.

Legend has it that if you go through the nose of the Buddha, you will be enlightened in the next life. My children were unimpressed, but not me. I had to have enlightenment. So I crawled on hands and knees through the Buddha's nostril only to get stuck at the point of exit. The other visitors were all there waiting to take a picture of their loved ones coming through the nostril. Instead, they were entertained by the sight of my behind coming through the Buddha's nose. Even from my breached position I could see the lights flashing from their cameras as my children pried me loose from the Buddha's nose. My only consolation was that when the other visitors laughed at me and told their stories, no one would be able to see my face.

75

Taking the Shinkansen to Tokyo, brought us from the very old to the very new. After traveling at almost 200 miles per hour, the ultra-modern look of Tokyo should not have come as a surprise. But I had glimpsed the majesty of Mount Fuji from the Bullet Train and found myself longing for its mystic beauty. The girls, however, were caught up in the thrill of youth. They, like the Japanese girls, strutted around in insanely high-heeled shoes and sang very bad karaoke.

The Japanese meals never disappointed. Presentation was always exquisite. One had the impression that each item was added with careful consideration. The food was neatly served and we enjoyed an abundance of sushi, rice, egg, noodles and other seafood dishes and meat dishes. Soba noodles, seafood, tonkatsu (fried pork cutlet) and omurice (an omelette rice dish) became a part of our daily language. The okonomiyaki or Japanese pizza engaged the palette with its combination of a flour batter, seafood (or meats of your choice) topped with seaweed flakes and Japanese mayonnaise. The revolving sushi restaurant made me wish I had a bottomless stomach so I could try every picturesque delicacy that rolled by me.

In the grocery stores and fish markets, Natasha was there to guide our choices. Even on our last night in Japan we were aware that the Japanese looked at us surreptitiously from behind their cell phones and newspapers. After all, we were in one of the most racially homogenous societies which boasted of about ninety-eight percent natives, and we are black. Yet, the Japanese sense of manners and dignity did not allow them to openly display their curiosity.

Not so in China. The aloof nature of the Japanese was replaced by people who gawked, openly took our pictures and touched our skin and hair without permission. Strange as it may seem, their curiosity turned out to be to our advantage. Once we de-planed and collected our bags, we realized we were in a pickle.

Alexandria and I had decided to visit China since there was no additional cost in airfare. Natasha was familiar with the country and culture but she had to work, so she stayed in Japan. We were on our own. In fact, we were alone without even the benefit of a common numbering system. Every sign was in Chinese and the woman at the information counter spoke only the most halting English. We were not in the country twenty minutes before we realized we could not even find our way to our hotel.

A couple of young men saw us huddled in front of the ticket machine at the train station looking very confused. They had compassion on us, bought our tickets and grabbed our bags indicating the open train. We, however, were not sure if we were being helped or robbed. Once the strangers boarded the train with our bags we had no choice but to follow. We spent several anxious minutes trying to keep our hands on our oversized bags and keep our balance while the train careened through the bowels of the Chinese earth.

Wangfuging Street is one of Beijing's most popular shopping streets but when we emerged from the belly of the train, the street stretched before us like a long and tightening noose. We acknowledged with sinking realization that our hotel could be anywhere on this street that was miles long. Our limited funds and lack of bargaining skills necessitated that we walk till we found our destination, but how far and in which direction? We couldn't even ask.

Alexandria had the foresight to copy an exact replica of our hotel address in Chinese characters. Once she retrieved it, we approached one of the many stern faced police officers patrolling the street. Speaking to an agent of the communist party was not my first choice; his impersonal demeanor conjured up images of Chinese prisons. But walking endlessly dragging two large suitcases seemed a more immediate death. Our anxiety regarding his response came to an anticlimactic end. He totally ignored us. If we were not standing in front of him, I would have sworn he could not see us. We took the cue and walked on, trying to decipher the numbers on Wangfuging Street. We got the attention of a passerby who read our paper and pointed down the long street, then walked away. At least we had a direction to go in. Now we just had to find the numeric character that matched the ones on our paper.

"Ich Nee San Shi," I began.

"Mom!" Alexandria said in an exasperated tone, "That is Japanese! It won't help us now!"

We walked slowly along the sidewalk down the crowded street trying to recognize the differences between the numbers on the store fronts. After walking for what seemed like miles, we stopped to compare our Chinese characters with the address of the nearest store. We examined the paper carefully trying to understand the characters. We were so engrossed that it took a few seconds to realize that there was a small crowd gathering. We froze wondering what was happening. We had attracted a small crowd. There were about a half a dozen people staring at us. Two were bolder than the others, they leaned over our shoulders and looked at our paper.

They spoke to each other in rapid Chinese then all began pointing in the same direction. After a stunned moment we realized they were directing us to our hotel. We were indeed on the right track. With an inadequate, "Thank you!" we set off at an encouraging pace.

We eventually found our hotel. Or should I say we found a faded worn out replica of the Internet version of our hotel? We looked at the luxurious hotel we had seen in the advertisements, then noticed the small alley beside it and realized that the sign for our hotel was at the end of that alley. To add to the insult, the hotel's façade was undergoing restoration so we were forced to drag our luggage through a construction zone to check in. The luxurious breakfast we anticipated consisted of cold greens, sprouts and beans with watery rice porridge and bad coffee. Our philosophy has always been to save money on accommodations and spend it on experience but this place tested the limits of our frugality.

Exploration of Wangfuging Street unearthed many small local businesses tucked between the expensive clothing stores. We enjoyed delicious Chinese food for pennies. One of those treasures was Serendipity Café. To our delight we could get simple sandwiches, hot beverages and free Wi-Fi.

We soon realized that traveling in Beijing without a guide was one of our less thought out moves. We have traveled internationally since Alexandria was two months old but nowhere in the western world had prepared us for China. Nor was China prepared for Alexandria.

A nineteen-year-old girl with shapely legs wearing short shorts or miniskirts and high-heels is sure to enjoy some male attention. Make that a black girl in the middle of Beijing and you are guaranteed a few accidents. Chinese men ran into poles as they stared at this exotic creature. Since I couldn't convince her to wear less conspicuous attire, I contented myself with a morbid satisfaction each time a man tripped or ran into a pole as he walked by my teenage daughter. I am sure that countless others suffered whiplash.

After a few days of having our pictures taken at random by complete strangers, our hair and skin touched unexpectedly by strangers and having women put their children next to us and insist on taking our picture, I was ready to hit someone. I glared at every person who raised a camera in our direction. I at least wanted to learn enough Chinese to tell them what I thought. Our little hand held translator was a miserable assistant. "Nee-haow" (Hello) and "Ting!" (Stop!), just weren't very helpful.

Alexandria was undaunted by the attention. In fact, she relished it. So when we met the rickshaw driver, he did not stand a chance.

The Chinese have a saying, "Have a mouth as sharp as a dagger but a heart as soft as tofu." Well, Alex hated tofu but daggers were pretty cool. We had settled into our little room and were now getting the hang of sightseeing. We walked through the streets of Beijing marveling at the street vendors selling bite-sized servings of caramelized fruit, raw meats, seafood, beetles and live scorpions on sticks. We were on our way to the Forbidden City. Once again, we underestimated the distance.

As we contemplated the walk to Tiananmen Square, a rickshaw driver approached us. He appeared to be a mature Chinese man of above average stature. He showed us a map of the Forbidden City and the ancient Chinese village surrounding it. The 1200 year old neighborhood was called a Hutong. The driver spoke no English but with gestures at his tattered map, he made it clear to us that he would give us a tour of the Hutong and take us to the Forbidden City for fifty kuai or yuan (about seven dollars US).

Due to the time, we did not want to go through the Hutong. So we began our negotiation for a direct ride to the Forbidden City. With gestures and shakes of our heads we bargained.
"Hutong No!"
"Forbidden City, Yes!"
"Fifty kuai No."
"Thirty kuai, Yes!"

The rickshaw driver was unwilling at first, shaking his head and insisting on fifty kuai but when we walked away, he relented. We again reiterated by pointing to his map and gesturing. "No Hutong!" He nodded his understanding. We climbed into the faded plush velvet two-seater, he mounted the bicycle and pedaled off.

Our first hint that we were off course was the deserted cobbled streets. We had stepped back into time. No longer were there cars or people in western garb. The buildings were made of stone with few visible openings. When the driver stopped and pointed to what appeared to be a metal ring for tying horses, we realized he had taken us to the Hutong. We again shook our heads and hands and said "No Hutong! Only Forbidden City!"

He simply ignored us and led us on a captive tour of the ancient streets chattering occasionally in Chinese to his captive audience. When he got off the bicycle and started pushing us up some stone steps, we became even more alarmed. We quickly dismounted and insisted once more, "Forbidden City!"

Finally, he seemed to concede and took us directly to the Forbidden City across from Tiananmen Square. I stretched out my hand to pay him the thirty kuai and he flatly refused. Using what appeared to be his only English word he said "Fifty kuai!"

Alexandria and I shook our heads in refusal and thus began the stand-off. The rickshaw driver was a fairly big guy and he seemed to grow with his fury. The rush of Chinese hit us like pellets and I began to remember why Tiananmen Square was so infamous.

I started to relent. "Alex, it's only a few dollars more…"

"No. It's the principle of it!" Alexandria insisted. She took the thirty kuai from my hand, walked up to the rickshaw driver, grasped his wrist, turned his palm over and slapped the money into his hand with the admonition, "Take it or leave it!"

She turned on her heels and walked away, leaving the astonished man, agape behind her. I was sure there was about to be another massacre so I gathered my druthers and ran after my child. "Are you nuts?!" I asked. "He is angry! He may have friends nearby…!" But she kept walking, head held high and resolute.

Seeing no one in hot pursuit, I said a quick prayer of thanks and returned to my pretense of being the adult in charge.

We toured much of the 183 acres of the world's largest palace, we hiked five miles along the magnificent Great Wall and toured the Beijing zoo; we beat off hecklers in the Pearl Market and bargained with the best in the Silk Market.

We watched a vendor slap a blind man who got in the way of her sale and we toured the Temple of Heaven but none of these wonders amaze me as much as my Alexandria.

The Great Wall of China

Who I Am

I am Beloved.
I am love.
I am faithful.
I am grateful.
I am moving stillness.
I am dancing voice.
I am rhythmic movement.
I am dynamic peace.
I am poetry in motion.
I am flowing Truth.
I am grace revealed.
I am practical wisdom.
I am freedom from fear.
I am Christ on the earth.
I am eternal;
And who are you?

∞

Years to come

Years to come
I'll be older
And wiser.
I will look back
With clear, dispassionate eyes
And the way will be obvious to me.
But for now I hobble along
Second guessing and regretting
My failings.
Never being fully here
Or all the way there.

∞

Lions and Tigers

Walking by faith as Abraham did
Is no bed of roses or picnic in the park.
There are many dangers revealed and hid.
Lions, tigers and bears prowl the dark.
Stepping out may take nerves of steel
But remaining on course is the real ordeal
There's an enemy waiting behind every tree,
But Lo and Behold! The enemy is me!

∞

Love's Beggar

Love has made a beggar out of me
Exposing my deepest aches
Eliciting from me secret hopes and dreams
Drawing out hidden desires.
"Please God…" I plead over and over
The pleas fall silently to the ground –
A tree falling in the great forest
No one hears its sound.

∞

Beyond Thought

Beyond the speaking of my mouth
There's the speaking of my mind
Beyond the speaking of my mind
Is the speaking of my heart
And fear intertwined.
Take me now to Silence.

∞

Farmhouse in Brittany, France

Letters from France, Part 1:

Hi Mom!

Good to hear your summer flower garden is blooming so nicely. Upload some pictures in your next email so I can see those beautiful sunflowers growing in front of your porch.

We arrived safely from the hustle and bustle of Paris to the French countryside in Brittany. Jean is restoring an old farmhouse she just bought so she welcomes the extra hands. We have swept and mopped from ground floor to attic. We ploughed a small patch of land next to the house and planted a variety of seeds. The children were not fond of the hard work but they are enjoying watching the little vegetable garden sprout. It is relaxing here in every way but one.

The remote little village is very picturesque. Jean actually bought the farmhouse from an elderly nun. There are more farm animals around than people. The neighbors are few and far between. They nod as they pass by. They seem to be friendly in that deep, earthy way.

A "Bonjour!" will get you an invitation for a glass of wine at ten in the morning. Once you enter their homes, these quiet folk will pull out their best glasses and platters and ply you with cheeses and other treats you can't pronounce. I find myself wishing fervently that I had at least dusted off those two college semesters of French and recovered the basics.

But the country side speaks in a language I can understand. You would love it here. There is such a glorious variety of flowers and wild plants! I go for a long run each morning. There are no hi-tech electronic security systems in the little village. The neighbors do not lock their doors. Crime is something they hear about on the news. In fact, the last time there was an outrageous affront was when a lady drove up to the front door of a neighbor's house in the middle of the night and put all of his potted plants into her car. He looked out the window at hearing the car. She looked up at him, smiled and waved, "Merci!" she yelled and with that, she drove away with his new plants.

The reason for the unfortunate man's loss is simple; he is not a farmer. In this area, all farmers have a very effective security system: the farmyard dog. He (the dog) has become the fly in the soothing ointment of my vacation.

The rolling hills, with the varying shades of green are so soothing. As I run, I can count on seeing a stately church steeple in the distance at the top of each hill. There are cattle in the fields interspersed with various crops. Beside my feet as I run are the lovely white blooms of Queen Anne's lace, bright yellow buttercups, fuchsia and purple Foxgloves and various other bold flowers whose name I do not know. But I have taken to going for my morning run along the country roads with a weapon in each hand.

As I run and walk, I listen out for the gurgle of the streams along the way. It soothes my heart like no other sound I know. I also listen out for another sound, the growl of the farmer's dog. These are not the pampered pets transported in purses. Nor are they the adorable animals we pet as we greet our neighbors back home. They are Herculean creatures bereft of a sense of humor and intolerant to the intrusion of the unfamiliar. There are no fences around the farmhouses and the front doors are often wide open. Those accursed animals have the run of the place and they are keenly aware of their power. On top of their position of authority, they are huge! German shepherds on steroids.

A few mornings ago there were two dogs, each coming at me from a different direction! I was certain I was about to be mauled. I was saved at the last minute by the appearance of the farmer's wife who calmly called to them in French. To my everlasting joy, they promptly heeded her call. By now, I know you are getting concerned for my safety but I have devised a plan.

Most of the dogs will back down with a stern yell from me. A few have become familiar with my passing and bark half-heartedly, turning tail at any sign of resistance, but there is one yard where reason has not prevailed. This yard is the focus of my offensive. There are very few loose rocks or sticks around the well-kept farmyards. I often run up a hill and round a corner only to hear the dreaded growl followed immediately by barking as the sound of my impending doom race toward me on four legs. I instinctively reach for a weapon but the yards and sidewalks are swept clean. I yell loudly to intimidate the beasts but I'm not sure how much longer that will work. So I have collected a few handy sized rocks and sturdy sticks that I keep in a pile outside the farmhouse in which I stay. I have also added a secret weapon to my plan.

So my plan, shaky as it seems, is to keep a rock in one hand and a stick in the other. I shake my fist showing my weapon when the mad animals begin their ferocious advance. So far, it's working... sort of. Yesterday, the first dog turned tail at the sight of my rock but the second would not yield. The farmer was a good distance away tending to his potatoes. And darn it, I can't even say "Help!" in French.

This morning, I put my plan into operation with confidence as I approached the home of the most aggressive brutes. I crested the hill and they crested the gate. I slowed to a cautious walk. They slowed to a stalking prowl. They growled with low pitched intimidation. I growled with a primal war cry. This was new to them. I could tell because they hesitated and looked at each other. What manner of beast was this? Emboldened by their momentary confusion I summoned the American pit bull in me. I growled again. This time it didn't work. Apparently I had gone too far. They charged. I threw a rock...and missed. They were unimpressed, now I could see the froth on the sides of their mouths as they closed the distance between us. I grasped my stick with shaking hands and swung wildly even before they were within reach. They slowed and began to encircle me, barking ferociously. I growled, yelled and swung with the insane desperation of a rabid animal.

We continued in this dance of death; they circled and barked, I swung and snarled. Then, I reached into my pocket and pulled out my secret weapon. I threw it directly at the dog closest to my stick. It landed in front of him with a plop. For an interminable moment, his bark deepened with ferocity. Then, he stopped and sniffed, moved closer and bit the object before him. Soon he was gnawing away like a puppy. His partner stood there confused. At first, he barked at the object with uncertainty, then at me. Finally, curiosity got the better of him and he moved in closer to get a better look at what had distracted his friend. That is when I threw the other half of my secret weapon. He skittered back in nervous alarm, then he approached the object before him. He sniffed, then he bit. Soon both dogs were on their haunches gnawing away at the strips of beef jerky I had thrown at them. I walked confidently by them, undisturbed.

So it's all good. I take the chance daily because the countryside is a healing balm. Some of the sweetest moments I have experienced here have been on these country roads. I find myself dancing in the middle of the deserted roads to Santana, the Bee Gees and the Spinners and other old school jams; my MP3 player strapped to my arm is like a trusted friend on my trips. There are about five cars per day on each country road. The children try to spoil my fun by reminding me that because there are so few cars, they fly around the corners with wild abandon. But believe me, I am now trained to hear the first thought of the farm dog *before* the growl, so I can hear a car in plenty of time.

I am considering taking the girls on a trip to the Valley of Kings. They want to tour large castles of the French nobility. It's a seven hour drive but after the quiet farm days, I think they are ready for some excitement.

Meanwhile, they are exploring the streams and ravines, riding the old donkey that was left behind and are enjoying the newfound novelties of country life.

As for me, with my new found plan, I am looking forward to going on my morning run...

Let me know how you are doing.

Love,

DAB

Countryside – Brittany, France

∞

Two Minutes

Two minutes to soothe my soul
Two minutes to change the world.
I sit beside this little pond
Eternity at hand
With obligations based on time.
So though eternity is mine,
All I have is
Two minutes then I'm back in time.

∞

91

Lord, Is Life Meant to Be So Hard?

*It's six a.m., I'm already running late
The alarm clock has sealed my fate.
Lord, I barely had time to pray
It's time to start another day.*

*No, pop tarts are not a healthy breakfast!
Okay – take them. Don't even toast them.
It's five minutes till eight, hurry or we'll be late!
Come on kids, don't play the fool
Remember you have to get to school.*

*Where's the homework? Here's the bus.
Please! Let's keep down the fuss.
Don't forget to ask the Lord to lead your day!
I'm already tired.
(I'm sure no one else feels this way.)*

*Say those reports are due when?
I have three other projects due then!
Lord, it would be really nice to get away and pray
But my break time has been sucked away.
Everything is overdue, Lord, how can I possibly rest?
Don't You see my office is a mess?*

*Get the kids, miss the gym
I can safely say I'm no longer thin.
Do your homework, get to bed
Or before you know it we'll be late again.*

Just Chasing the Sun

Finally, Lord, time with only You.
Okay, I'll take that call, I know they need me, too.
Well, Lord, I tried to read Your Word each chance I got
I even witnessed quite a lot.

I encouraged someone to pray
You ministered to another in Your own way.
You used me Lord, that I can now see.
But what will become of me?
When will I finally be set free?

'It's My peace that sets you free
No matter what the problems might be.
Look to Me and you will see,
It's My peace that sets you free.'

The answer lies in what's Eternal
God's light is more than diurnal
I'll let this mold my attitude each day.
Then the Lord Almighty will be my stay.

∞

When I'm By Myself

When I'm by myself
I have very few faults
I find that I am witty, fun-loving, and smart.
I think constantly of others
And the things that I could share
For my fellow man I've even shed a tear.

I find that I am quiet, introspective and wise.
I find that life's interesting so much to do
And think and feel...
It really holds quite an appeal.

When I'm by myself
I find I wish with all my heart
To live for God and do my part.
Oh, if only my friends could see
The "me" I see
When I'm by myself.

∞

Dying Embers

Embers of emotions dying
A faint glow on an empty
And distant stage.

The best of me
A soliloquy
Without an audience.

No rules, no lines
Just memories of dreams
And dust to clean from an empty stage
Where I am a distant memory.

∞

Welcome, Loneliness

My companion is here:
Welcome Loneliness.
Why do men complain about your company?
You are a friend of God.

Like the dark, you hold unseen treasures.
People rejoice and fellowship in the light
But it's in the dark, it is in loneliness
That we find the light in our hearts;
The Comforter who cannot be seen or touched;
So come sweet Loneliness, let us walk together.
Tell me of how you kept my Lord's company
When He walked the earth.

Tell me of the broken-hearted and downtrodden
That have learned strength from you.
Pour into my heart the sweet wine of your communion
So I can share the cup of my Lord.
Break bread with me so I can share the fellowship of
His sufferings.

Yes, come sweet Loneliness,
I would not trade your company for many false
lights and fleeting comforts.
Your company is His ministry to me
My Lord has sent you, so welcome, sweet friend.

∞

Tours, France

Letters from France, Part 2:

Hi Mom,

I am happy to hear you are missing us! (Smile). We miss you, too, and wish you were here. It sure is nice to have email access to you again. We have to seek out Internet connection on our low budget vacation.

Jean's farmhouse in Brittany is quaint but the kids seemed a little bored with no television, spotty Internet service and only farm work to do all day. So Saturday morning I packed up all four kids with lots of snacks and we set off on an adventure. Jean did not want to stray too far from her new home so I took her three kids with us for a weekend of visiting castles. My Alexandria is the eldest of the four girls and the only one of us who has a clue how to speak a word of French. The youngest one is twelve and all heads turn when a boy walks by.

They have actually devised a directional system to tell each other when they spot a cute boy. Someone will yell out "Twelve o'clock!" This apparently random interest in time is a cover for locating a boy based on the hands of an analog clock.

This is my first time away from the safety of Jean's significant knowledge of the French, their language and culture. She has been very informative on the most mundane of facts. Still, some things are bound to slip through the cracks. I left her my small rental car for which I was specifically instructed in English to fill with "Ninety-five no lead gaz." Her slightly larger car was a better fit for the five of us. What she forgot to tell me was that it takes only diesel fuel.

So off we went with a dictionary, a map and a first year French student for our seven hour drive to the city of Tours in the Loire Valley. I am told the kings and nobility of France cavorted there and we will find the luxuries of a bygone era.

I have decided that the French are a very dramatic lot. You are wondering why I've made such a seemingly rash judgment. Well, here's the reason; we were driving down the highway and the signs started saying, "Danger...." I asked Alexandria, "What does it say?" She read the sign and told me, "It says *'Danger of Death* ...''

I told her with some urgency, "Alexandria we are going at 130km per hour, please tell me exactly what the rest of the warning signs are saying!"

Alexandria replied in a frantic voice, "Mom, I don't know, I can't understand the rest of the French!" I immediately slowed down to avoid eminent death. But we kept going. The miles passed and there was nothing but smooth sailing.

I wondered, *Hmm, now let's see, we have over 400 miles to go, should I slow down, pull over and get the dictionary? Naah, other motorists are whizzing by, the highway looks clear and I don't see the point in pulling over when we will be none the wiser.* So we kept going. It was just as well. It turned out it was simply a warning about driving too closely behind other vehicles, or something like that (we think). Such a dramatic sign for routine safety rules. I wonder if that's how the French feel reading our safety signs along the Florida Turnpike.

Anyway, we stopped half way to Tours, in a city called Nantes, and went into the local McDoh (That's the nickname for McDonald's in France). Turned out, it was the first time I saw any meal for under one euro! When we got back to the car, it would not start. Two guys finally reacted to the raised hood and came over. One had his shirt off and the other was trying to flirt a bit with the teen girls. I was exasperated. I wondered, "Do they think we care a rat's rear how charming they look if we can't understand what they're saying and we are stranded???" But I was alone in my opinion. The girls blushed and gushed and offered random phrases.

Ironically, a tow truck driver pulled up and parked his truck two spaces over from us. But Alexandria's French was limited to "Tombar une pain." Which she thought meant we broke down (or we are having back pain). So we didn't know how to ask a professional for help. He disappeared into the McDonald's before we could figure out an approach. We were stuck with the friendly guys who looked busy but seemed to know nothing. Eventually, one of the guys pump what I think is the carburetor, saying "bad gaz." He pumped it repeatedly and the car eventually started running again. At this point, we had been driving for about three hours. We were almost half way to the Loire Valley. We decided to keep going. So with this blissful ignorance, we resumed our journey to the Valley of the Kings.

We made it into Tours, in the Loire Valley much later than we planned. We arrived after eight p.m. on Saturday and everything was closed. The car sputtered to a stop and I coasted to the side of the street. Turned out, we broke down in front of a sex shop, but that was good! The car rental agency we used had a branch directly across the street from the sex shop. The girls were more interested in the sex shop than the car rental agency. Fortunately, the sex shop was closed. Unfortunately, the car rental office was also closed until Monday. It also turned out these shops were linked to a major train station so vagrants were all around and we had no place to stay.

The girls were calm and obedient. Alexandria and I walked down the streets checking at hotels with her smattering of French while the other three stayed locked in the car. We checked the more reputable hotels first. At ninety-five euros a night for two people, we were NOT staying at the Best Western. So down the ladder of quality we slid with each step. There were no signs indicating public restrooms. Eventually, we each took turns inquiring about a room while a second person snuck into a restroom because we all HAD to go and they wouldn't let us use their facilities unless we were staying at the hotel.

Finally, we turned to a rundown looking building that was reminiscent of the one we dubbed "El Dumpo" the last time we were in France. (We didn't know the French word or its Spanish equivalent for dump, so we made up our own.) They offered us two small adjoining rooms for a total of 131 euros a night and a note to put on our car that MAY prevent it from getting towed. We couldn't read the note but Alexandria surmised it said the car belongs to guests of the hotel.

The hotel is actually decent considering our budget. It has Internet. (Yeah!) So I am currently in the lobby typing you this email on a dusty ancient computer. The girls are taking turns getting well needed showers after our nine hour trip. The room has a 2x2 shower and a little toilet. There is no air conditioning and we are at the top on the fifth floor. The girls can now attest to the scientific principle that hot air rises. Fortunately, we can open the large windows. There are no screens but with five people in cramped quarters, we are desperate for some fresh air. The gnats started biting us as soon as we opened the first window but they're not too bad. There is a sedative for the kids—a TV. At their age, everything is all one big adventure so there is no complaining. The noises on the street below are somehow reassuring. We are safe and warm (very warm).

This is the Valley of Kings, but so far, we have arrived like peasants. But not to worry, we have Internet and snacks and there is the beaconing light of McDoh across the street so the children feel at home. Our plan is to visit the great castles and chateaux in the Loire Valley dating back to the fifteenth century. There is the Chateau Ambroise, Chateau Chenonceau and about thirty more including the home of Leonardo Da Vince (a must see). There are seemingly endless trains and tours to castles and vineyards. If my calculations are correct, we can visit the castles of the French nobility and still have money for two decent meals each day. Cheap fast food will fill the gaps. The car can wait until Monday. The children are content with the plan. Even as I type, they are upstairs falling asleep under the glow cast by the beaconing arches from McDoh across the street. It will take me a little longer to adjust to our slightly smelly room. But such are the joys of a shoestring vacation.

Chenonceau Castle- Loire Valley, France

Here

Here is a multi-layered place; a multi-faceted orb.

Here is the beginning of awareness,
Deepening into infinity.

Here is layered with the pain of reality
The outer skin of divinity.
The pain of reality...
We shrink from the pain,
But in it we find our true selves.
In it is the door to Presence.

Here is where we dare to be ourselves
If we dare to be truly Here.

Not running to the next place, the next goal
The next thought, just being, and allowing ourselves
To be truly Here.

∞

Joy

Joy has stepped in on the spring breeze
She is peeking out from behind the bushes
She is whispering from the trees
I hear her in my mother's throaty laughter
And see her in my daughters' smiles.
I'm opening my doors to welcome her
I think I'll sit with her for a while.

∞

Mosquito Mystique

How does a tiny mosquito know
How to find the very spot I cannot see
And sting me?
How does it calculate the length of my arms
And find the space on my back that I cannot
Easily reach, giving itself time to flee?
Do you find this amazing or is it just me?
When I wait in stillness, it is far away
When I move it darts out of my way.
When I get the spray,
It stays at bay.
A brain smaller than the bump it leaves on my skin
Yet able to outsmart me and leave me itching.
An insect's smarter than me? It cannot be.
That kind of intelligence lives in me
I'm sure of it; it has to be.
It is in a realm I cannot see
But I'm sure it's available to me.

∞

Night Gown

The night floats faithfully
Down upon the earth
Like the donning of a well-worn negligee.

The earth stretches up to greet her
Through its tree-like arms
And she flows gracefully
To touch cool soil beneath.

A familiar gown
That whispers,
"Sleep well"
to all who can still hear
her soft command.

∞

Redemption

From the dark, deep depths of madness I came.
Slowly, hesitantly, as a babe unwilling to take his first step;
Painfully wishing I could remain in this madness
Remain in this self-possessing whirl, which kept me from myself.

Yes, from myself, and from all around me.
From the jeering smiles, the pitying glances and the sharp words
that cut at my breast like a jagged saw.

But I came.

I came from the unearthly haze of insanity
To the rough ragged roads of my reality.

I could think clearly now,
And I wished with all my heart
I hadn't done it.

But rage was within me then!

And it had flowed like the warmth of a beloved friend.
But when the act was done the feeling fled like a hunted hare.

And my soul screamed with the anguish of its empty pain.

I longed for a jeer or even a tear
To fill the void and ease the pain.

Then in the deep silence of my soul
I heard a voice, sweet and low.

There were no words in its deep call,
Yet my soul became enthralled.

Just Chasing the Sun

Urged beyond my wall of doubt
I found a strange new world without.
It had no walls that I could see, only images of me.

Faced with the mirror of my eternal soul,
I thought to cringe or even flee,
Such were the sins I thought I'd see.

But it was washed in crimson Blood
Which came in torrents like a flood.
And when in awe I looked closely,
All I could see was a brand new me!

∞

The Toast

I often get lost in Natasha's eyes; big soft brown eyes that sparkle invitingly. They have captivated me from infancy. Even when she developed that winning smile, her eyes remained the magnet for my soul. Your first child is always an introduction to amazement; a miracle starting in the deepest reaches of your very own being and continuing to amaze you as she grows. Of course, every mother feels this way, so why reminisce?

This was my daughter's wedding day. On this particular day, the transformation I have watched from a front row seat all these years will be complete, or at least it will crest and evolve. It was my job to deliver the toast but what could I, who had failed at marriage, tell a couple starting out?

I watched my little princess step into a stunning gown and walk softly down the aisle to her waiting prince, Takeshi, wearing a haori hakama, the traditional wedding dress of his culture. The fairytale has become her reality.

We must have looked at hundreds of wedding dresses, I watched her try on a dozen and I knew exactly what she was going to wear. I even helped her with a last minute emergency repair to her attire. But when she walked out on her father's arm in that white satin ball gown with its sweetheart neckline and delicately beaded appliqués, I was just as wowed as the guests who were seeing her in a wedding dress for the first time. But it wasn't always harps and joy.

At three, she stole a candy bar from a store and learned through the ire of her parents never to steal again.

At ten, I finally had to rescue her sister from her tyrannical reign.

At twelve, she raced back into the house convinced she was being chased by a large bull. Her passion for fantasy novels had transformed the trash can into a charging beast in the predawn light as she waited for the bus in our quiet suburban neighborhood.

At fifteen, she defied my every word.

I am told I pulled over on the Interstate and ordered her out of the car. (I am sure I would never do such a thing.) However, I freely admit threatening to kill her in the kitchen of our home, and I meant it. Behind those soft and sparkling brown eyes lay a stubbornness that reached legendary proportions in her teens.

For ten minutes, we stood toe-to-toe, neither one backing down.

For one insane moment, I was convinced that reason had been strangled by my child and violence was my only choice. I was sure no jury of my peers would have convicted me. After all, there would be a few mothers on that jury with rebellious teens of their own.

Natasha's was that seething type of rebellion, like an earthquake that rumbles from the belly of the earth right before it cracks the soil under your feet and swallows you whole. The chubby legs, adorable curls and quick smile gave way to legs that kicked soccer balls and legs that took confident steps across the collegiate stage.

At first, those legs wobbled too much for comfort as she held her baby sister for the first time, then walked more confidently to the bus stop alone for the first time, they boldly boarded the transcontinental liner as she flew unaided to China.

We struggled through her insistence that Moses wrote the Pentagon (instead of the Pentateuch); through her stripping the gears (and my nerves) in my stick shift Toyota as I taught her to drive.

We struggled with her talking back to me while in the hills of Austria as she refused to iron her wrinkled shirt. She insisted on looking like a homeless vagabond in a strange country and I insisted that surely a three-week vacation in Europe obligated your children to some small obedience.

My little girl had moved through life with the determination that belied her name. She had grown and matured and it was with bittersweet joy that I recognized that so must I.

I am not known for being at a loss for words but I was clueless as to how I would toast the essence that has captivated my heart as she merged with another. But life was working diligently to provide clarity through the pain of circumstance.

The beauty of my daughter's heart was reflected in her guest list. It could have been a roll call for the United Nations. Having lived in Asia for the last few years, she accumulated friends of every continent and persuasion.

Her groom, Takeshi, is Japanese and this meant his family would be flying seven-thousand miles to bear witness to the union. But the crucible that is stress has a way of offering us tests which become defining moments in our lives. Unbeknownst to us, a storm was getting ready to test the young couple before the vows were offered up to Heaven.

At 2:30 in the morning I was a front seat witness to one of those deciding moments. My daughter and her fiancé discovered that his brother and sister-in-law were stranded in one of the largest international airports in the world.

Add the fact that neither of the two visitors spoke functional English and they had the further questionable luck of being separated from each other, and you have the elements of a storm.

Add my hotheaded daughter and her stubborn fiancé as the helpless onlookers, aware that the couple was stranded and separated from each other but unable to find them or help them, and the crucible is set with all the elements of a perfect storm.

Their cell phones wouldn't work so they couldn't find each other and we couldn't find them. If they managed to find each other in the airport, the next possible flight might get them in town in time for the wedding but the weather held even that possibility hostage.

I fluttered and fretted like a mother hen whose nest had been disturbed. I wanted to help but I was unprepared for the level of complexity in the problem they faced. So I was forced into the position of helpless onlooker. My daughter did not turn to her mom. Nor did she lose her cool.

In this crucible of stress, these two young people remained calm and pulled together until the crisis was over. They literally put their heads together, and with a laptop between them, they problem solved for hours. They eventually located the couple, connected them with help in the airport and ensured their flight for the wedding day; all without a harsh word between them.

And so I was given the substance of my toast. After the vows were made, I witnessed to the lesson I had learned and offered them this summary...

Handling crises: That's what marriage is all about. We all love to celebrate the good times but it's how we handle the crises that will decide the strength and quality of a marriage. But if we are brave enough to face the truth, we will admit that marriage is much more about handling problems and disasters than it is about romance and special moments.

It is in the crucible of stress that we really find out if we are a team or not; if we even like each other or not. Those are the deciding moments. I told my daughter and new son-in-law, handle all your crises like the team you were at two a.m. Friday morning and you will beat all odds. And yes, you will have plenty of special moments like this one, too.

Use those times to deliver those grandbabies I'm so looking forward to spoiling. I know they'll look just like you.

(I Corinthians 13)

Love Will Not Fail

Be patient, Beloved, your Lover is breaking the sound barrier
to reach you.
He will not fail.
He will die to reach you and He already has;
Therefore, death, the final barrier has been destroyed.
He lives forever, He cannot fail.
So don't despair of the valleys and the boulders that separate us.
Don't faint at your own feeble feelings.
There's a mighty Love coming to your rescue!

Fear?
Can't you see it fleeing like a frightened dog with its tail between
its legs?
Fear is afraid! Ha!
Shame?
Where is it? Behold you are in the light and are unashamed!
Doubt?
It is being crushed by the slow sure steamroller of My Love.
Excess?
Have I not promised I will cleanse you?
Have I not given you purity in place of bad habits?
Don't allow your old lovers in, make no room for Impatience.
Do not hold hands with Pride.
Dive into pains, the travails of your life.
Dive deep and you will find Me there, loving you.
Tell Despair he is not welcome.
Let Stress find you looking into My eyes!
Let Suffering find you rejoicing.
My love is yours, I want every part of you and I will not be denied!
Yield now, I will not force, so yield now, Beloved.

Erotic Love

What if the Apple wasn't an apple at all
But a man named Adam, dark, handsome and tall?
What if the story of the Garden of Eden
Held a mystery that has remained hidden?
What if the devil saw that God's love was his ultimate defeat
So he decided to invent a counterfeit?
Oh, it would look just like the real thing
But with passion, lust and jealousy dropped in.
It would start out innocent
Just like the Love that's from Heaven sent
But your focus of attention would move from God's salvation
To your new sensation.

Then it would grip you just like an addiction
Sealing your fate like a court conviction.
And for a special twist of pain
Mary will love John but John will love Jane.
For the few who make it through these steps
Add some boredom and a few extra debts
Until there's nothing of that romantic love left.
Unlike the real thing, this love will fade
But you won't know the difference until the price is paid.
Now for the final touch;
Make it so tempting you'll want it so much
You'll fall headlong in love without even consulting the One above
Then you will unwittingly trade your God given gift
Perfect and whole
For the one from the devil
The one made of stone.
So keep this in mind before you jump in
And inquire of Jesus if it's the real thing.

∞

113

Become a Thief

Become a thief
And steal your life back from the jackals
That encircle you,
Telling you what you must do before you can rest.
Snatch back bits of time from the
Taskmaster called Busyness.
Refuse the shiny baubles offered to entertain
And steal back the treasures of your own silence.
Stop being a good slave to the system of death
Be in bold and constant rebellion against
The status quo
Become a thief
And steal back the gift you lost.

∞

In The Now

IF You had told me that True Love
Has nothing to do with "the perfect mate"
And is all about loving You, I would have turned aside,
But not now.

If You had told me that to have passion and desire
Means to suffer
I would have turned aside,
But not now.

If You had told me that to hope
Is to risk disappointment in this life
I would have ceased from hoping,
But not now.
If You had told me that to gain Heaven

114

Just Chasing the Sun

Means losing all I want on earth
I would have turned aside,
But not now.

If You had told me all this, I would not have heard
My ears were filled with my own hopes and fears.

Now I ask You, place within me Your love
Your passion and desire
Your hope, your vision of Heaven.

Unstop my ears, disperse my fears
And cause me to hear all You have to tell me
In the Now.

∞

Love is a River

It is said we never step in the same river twice
And Love is a River, ever flowing, ever new.

When we bathed together in that River,
I didn't know it. I thought it only a pool.
I didn't know love, I didn't know you.

The River washes away regrets, it cleanses and renews.
If I could be that River, I'd wash and refresh you.

Released from the stagnant pools where I've dwelt for years
Letting go of judgments, freed from fears
I wash the tears you never shed
And offer you this place instead:

A placid place, a River new
To look within at all that's True.

∞

South African Sunrise

"There are two South Africas and the Coloureds straddle them in an uncomfortable balance."

Banny's well-modulated, heavily accented voice traveled across the plush fabric seats to reach the listeners in the rear of the tour bus. "Apartheid taught us to hate each other. And the hate lives on in the form of fear and prejudice." He paused as the driver slowed so the tourists could take in the majesty of Table Mountain, complete with its canopy of clouds descending in the iconic "tablecloth" formation.

The tour bus had traveled along the peninsula earlier that morning and the sightseers had soaked up the beauty and contrast of the Twelve Apostles mountain range and the Atlantic Ocean. Now they headed inland to explore the history, culture and daily life of the Townships of Cape Town, South Africa.

"Apartheid; apartness, became the official policy of our country in 1948. By this, Whites and Blacks were separated and Blacks were disenfranchised and dehumanized. Later today, we will visit the site of the famous District Six where an entire community was forcibly moved out of their homes and businesses. In all, 60,000 people of color were displaced from desirable areas of Cape Town to the Cape Flats where there was nothing but wind, sand and flatlands." Banny paused for emphasis.

"Today 2.1 million of Cape Town's five-million people live in these townships in the Flats. The policy of Apartheid ended in 1994, yet its gaping wounds are still obvious in the contrast between the townships and the cities. But as the sun rises each day, so does hope. You will see it in the midst of the townships. But you don't have to look that far. Hope is here on this bus. We are riding together, freely; you White and me Black."

He flashed a smile, softening the spear point of his words. Banny told the story of South Africa in what he considered unembellished truth. Yet, he was never offensive. His charm disarmed his listeners. And when he smiled, which was often, men and women on the tour bus were left with the feeling you get when you finally catch a glimpse of the sun for the first time on a dreary day.

He was a handsome fellow with pecan brown skin, wide cheek bones and dark sparkling eyes. His prominent nose and full lips held a sensuous hint of arrogance. He knew his script well and why shouldn't he? After all he was South Africa. He had been born in the abject poverty of the flats, weaned on a dirt floor and ran barefoot in the streets. He had bathed at the water pipes beside the road and carried water home on his head as a young boy much the same way the women did now as they rode by them in their air conditioned luxury coach with him describing the scene for his passengers.

In fact, from time to time, he saw people he knew as he was describing their existence from behind the tinted windows. They would often look up from plying their wares or washing their clothes on the side of the road and wave. They couldn't see him but they knew he was there. Banny had made it big in the eyes of his childhood friends. He had managed to complete his college education while they still sought a foothold in this post-Apartheid system.

He was from the township of Langa (Xhosa for sun). He was Zulu like his fathers before him. He was descended from the blood lines of the great Shaka Zulu himself. The drum beat of greatness still echoed faintly in his heart. His mother, however, was Xhosa and would not be denied. The conflict between the two tribes seemed to culminate in the union between his mother and father. His father was a modern man with progressive aspirations for his people and his continent. He often attended the local political gatherings. His mother held fast to the power of tradition and the dealings of the spirit world.

Their relationship could not sustain the rift in ideologies. His father left long before his Abakhwetha.

When Banny was sixteen-years-old his body had been covered with white clay, he and a small group of his friends had been taken out into the bush and left to survive on their wits for three months. He had not just survived, he had thrived. His mother, Ndosa, had worried about him then. She had tried to sneak food to him but he, considering that cheating, had rejected all contact. He would become a man on his own terms. He would face the spirit world and have them learn *his* name.

After the paint had worn off and his three months were over, his mother had searched anxiously for him. He had not immediately returned home and she had begun to fear the worst. She had gathered his uncles and his cousins and they had searched frantically for him. They had cared then. They had found him, to their amazement, in the shelter of a thatched hut he had built for himself with a wild pig roasting over a wooden fire. His body had grown robust and strong, unlike his emaciated peers who had struggled to find food. He had amassed a collection of carvings he had made during the long spring nights and his mother had treasured them for many years.

In those days, his mother had told of his survival with pride and Banny would always say it was the morning sun that had strengthened him. His friends always laughed but the elders would nod in quiet rhythm. Yet, his manhood rite of passage was not in itself an exceptional event. All his friends boasted of their ordeals. Some of his Xhosa friends had died from their circumcision rites. Death hunted every person he knew, including him, with unrelenting vigilance.

His tour groups were generally unaware of the underbelly of South African life. They were here to see the other South Africa. They were here for the beauty of Table Mountain, the rolling lushness of the Winelands and the amazing expanse of the Cape of Good Hope.

They sought the powerful swells of the ocean surf; the unfamiliar tastes of seafood from two oceans and sightings from land and sea of lions, baboons, seals and great whites. They sought the superficial emblems of hope of a South Africa brought into their consciousness by the struggle against racial injustice; a noble theme. And he was happy to oblige.

The beauty and varied span of choices in activity and observations left him with countless ways to enthrall, entertain and make money. He worked for a tour company throughout the week, then worked privately on the weekends making a week's salary in two days on his own.

The tour bus pulled into a dusty parking lot in the township of Langa. As they disembarked, Banny encouraged the passengers to taste the sheep meat, buy locally made beadwork and to visit the nearby traditional healing center. He watched the tourists step into the sunshine and look around in a daze. He never tired of watching the reactions of visitors as they acclimated to the shanty town around them. He led them into a ramshackle box without windows covered by a corrugated roof. The doorway hinted of the clutter within and the scents that wafted out were strangely unidentifiable to the visitors. Just inside the door, one could see skins of various animals dangling from the ceiling and a shadowy figure moving about.

A few members of the group refused to enter. Banny, prepared for this common eventuality, re-directed them to the make shift arts center two doors down. Tapps, the driver, always stayed within a stone's throw of the tour bus and watched his passengers like a mother hen with her brood. So Banny was free to roam.

With twenty minutes for himself he quickly made his way through the street vendors of roasted sheep heads, cell phones and black market designer knock offs. He slipped into the one bedroom Mandela house to find his friend, Witness, sharpening the blades of an ancient looking pair of shears. "Man, what you doing here?" They

120

clasped hands and embraced. Banny took a furtive look around the crowded room. Witness caught his eye and was immediately defensive. "We can't all have big jobs and live in the city like you, Man." Banny did not respond. The silence held a pain that melted Witness' defensiveness.

"You need a quick trim? This thing is the sharpest tool in the trade, Man!"

"Yah. Yah, clean me up, quick as you can." Witness grabbed a plastic covering from the recesses of the tent and went to work as Banny sat down.

"Where de folks?"

"The kids in school, Sanfi is selling phone cards around the corner and you know her mother is at her usual spot selling sheep head."

Seven people lived in the one-room house. The four children walked to the public school several blocks away and the three adults hustled daily to supplement the pittance Sanfi received from the government. Witness had climbed the light pole across the street and managed to hook the family house up to the electricity but there was only one light bulb that struggled against the darkness.

As Witness clipped away at Banny's hair, he asked hesitantly, "Man, you been doing okay?" They had all heard the rumors but Banny had been his friend since they were toddlers running barefoot in the streets. He could not forsake his friend.

"Yah. I'm fine. I'm fine." He jumped up so quickly Witness just missed gouging him with the shears.

"How much I owe you, Man?"

"Man, you know you don't have to pay me." They both knew the

121

words were just a formality. Even as he said it, Banny was pressing a wad of rands into Witness' hand. He grabbed the plastic covering and quickly dusted off his customer. His eyes having accustomed themselves to the dimness could see hair clipping as if they were standing in the sunlight.

Banny darted out of the darkness and away from the questions. His feet traced the familiar path to his friend Ludumo's house but the make-shift door closed as he approached, plunging his heart into a darkness more real than the one he'd just left behind in his friend's house.

He made it back to the tour bus as his passengers started to wend their way back to its air conditioned comfort. They were oblivious of his neatened appearance. Their arms were filled with carvings, medicinal powders, beads and other emblems of Africa. Their eyes were filled with the wonder of poverty and survival.

On the way to District Six, Banny fell easily into the role of eloquent tour guide but his heart was bleeding from the slight of the closed door and the veiled implications of Witness' words. Not too long ago, he was an undisputed celebrity in town. But it was at the expense of his heart because he had been living a lie.

Ironically, now that they knew the truth, he again had to forfeit his heart. Either way, his life was filled with pain. He explained to his charges that the first heart transplant was performed at the hospital they could see from their window. Silently, he wondered if anything could heal the break in his own heart.

Having dropped his charges back at their hotels, Banny rode with the bus driver to their checkout station. He slipped into his street clothes and sprinted across the street in time to hop on the city bus. The contrast of going from luxury and authority to jerky fits and starts and anonymity always jarred him. But he was beginning to find solace in anonymity. It meant freedom from judgment. No one turned their back or moved away from him when he rode the city bus. He knew no one, he was no one.

He dashed up the four flights of steps to his tiny apartment and stepped in to its cool, neat, sparsely furnished interior. He hung his keys on the hook and gratefully slipped off his shoes. He could smell the aroma of dinner as he rounded the corner. Never stood with his back to him, shirtless, as he juggled a meal in full swing unaware of Banny's entry. Beads of sweat rolled down the small of his back as he moved between the oven and the counter in an effort to assemble the meal. Banny paused and took in the sight. He took a deep breath, felt his heart surge as if in answer to its own pain.

"Hey." He said softly.

Never spun around in surprise, then greeted him with a wide smile. "Hey, yourself." They embraced for a long moment. Then, Never extricated himself with a breathless, "Wait till you see what I have for dinner."

They had lived this way for over a year now. At first, they had used all the obvious excuses, citing savings and convenience as the reason for sharing a one-bedroom apartment. After the overcrowding of the township homes, this arrangement should have gone unquestioned. But Banny's mother had shown up unannounced and invited herself to spend the night. Not known for tact or diplomacy, she had gone into the bedroom uninvited.

With the instinct born of experience, she had come to the conclusion that her son was sharing more than living space and had left the apartment, scandalized. She could not contain her hurt and outrage and within a fortnight, Banny found himself shunned, insulted and ostracized by almost everyone he knew in his old township. The few people who still showed him friendship or respect were mostly those in other townships who had not yet felt the winds of vengeful gossip.

So he was no longer living a lie. His heart had been laid bare but had been crushed by the loss of community that accompanied the disclosure. He enjoyed the solace of home life only after moving three times to prevent his mother from targeting his home with her religious fervor. He threw himself into work when not at home. He buried his dreams of greatness under the safety of anonymity. He would have lived and died in obscurity had it not been for one incident. It happened on a grey and foggy evening in an old and dowdy township on the outskirts of Zululand.

It had been a typical day in the Cape. Nondescript in the minds of South Africans raised in its beauty, the sun had glistened over the ocean and the rolling hills undulated in verdant green. He had guided a tour outside the city and was drained from a day of catering to the needs and questions of forty-five first time visitors. They, in turn, had taken in all they could of tribal history, rituals and culture. The juxtaposition of old and new left them trying to reconcile both worlds. Most of the passengers had fallen into a light doze as the tour bus wended its way through the township. The carpet of fog had descended much the same way the clouds descended and blanketed Table Mountain each afternoon.

But this fog thickened with malevolent intent as it prowled through the lowlands. It was thirsty for a victim and the lights of the oncoming bus met that need.

Tapps, was a very conscientious driver. He was a small, thin man with angular features. He barely made the height requirement to drive the bus but he handled it like a chef wielding a filet knife. He hardly spoke and kept his hands on the wheel and his eyes on the road like a sentinel at his post. He had driven diligently all day along Route Sixty-two.

They had toured fruit farms, explored wine orchards; viewed majestic vistas of lowlands and mountain passes and passed through countless small villages. Now night had fallen as they headed back to Cape Town. The group of forty-five tourists were all exhausted and in various stages of sleep. Tapps sat across from Banny as they had on many long tours, handling the wheel like a carved sentinel.

This night was a little different though. Tapps' had taken his wife to hospital the night before. She had been expecting their first child and was long overdue. It had been a long and arduous labor. The baby was born in the wee hours of the morning, a bellowing big headed boy. Tapps felt ten-feet tall when he left the hospital just before sunrise. But he didn't have time for a nap. He barely had time for a shower and had made it to the check in point one- minute before his shift was scheduled to start.

The trip took them deep into Zululand outside the range of cell phone towers and was compounded with unexpected detours. So after twelve hours on the road, he was struggling to stay focused on the path of light his headlights cut into the blackness of this unfamiliar route.

He rounded an unexpectedly sharp corner and there was the fog, fangs bared and dripping. It covered the road and stood erect in a towering pillar of impenetrable fear, daring man or machine to pass through it. Tapps' usually lightning fast reflexes were a split second off as his sleep deprived mind struggled to grasp the layout before him. Did the road continue to curve or go straight? He did not know and he could not see.

The fog, seeing the opening made by doubt, leapt into his mind and fear seized him like a steel trap. Fearing what he could not see, he swung the steering wheel violently to the left. The passengers awoke with violent screams as their bodies were suddenly flung to the left. Tapps let out a bloodcurdling yell of fear as his eyes finally focused and he saw the giant baobab tree rapidly coming at him. He swung the wheel again. The image of his bellowing big headed baby boy filled his mind; then all went black.

There was stillness in Zululand until the predawn light chased the fog away. The sunrise filtered through the trees until it found the scene of the wreck. The tour bus lay on its side like a defeated animal. There was no sign of life. So the sun searched the underbrush until it lit upon Banny. He had been thrown from the vehicle and had landed in the tall grass. "Get up little chief. There is work to do," the sun echoed, and Banny stirred as if from a dream.

He sat up only to gasp in pain at the effort and flop back into the weeds. His entire body was on fire as if the sun had gotten into his blood and was burning him from inside. Now fully awakened by the pain, he groaned and groped for his right shoulder. He grasped it and found the source of his agony. "Get, up little chief, there's work to do." He gathered himself and stood up.

His body was bloody and ached all over but his shoulder commanded his full attention. At least it did until he caught sight of the bus a few yards from him. He quickly comprehended the scene. He had not been wearing a seat belt and had been thrown from the bus when it hit the tree. But Tapps, the tourists, where were they? His feet took off as if by an alien power and his legs raced faster than his mind. He reached the bus and, his injuries forgotten, leapt unto a felled branch, then unto the right front tire.

The glass in the door had been shattered where he had been ejected. The force of the impact had forced it open and warped the frame. He kicked at the door with unwavering determination until it slid off track and caved into a type of crude staircase into the overturned bus. He stepped down into the wreckage as the sun rose and gently shone its light on the scene within.

Bodies were strewed all over the interior of the vehicle. Some lay over the sides of the upturned seats, some were against the windows, which were now the floor of the bus. Some were even on top of each other three persons deep. Tapps lay slumped against the driver's window, his head blooded, and his body unmoving. Banny yelled his name but there was no reaction. He shook him but Tapps did not move. His body was partially wedged between the steering wheel and the seat. Banny did not think. He did not allow the fear of the horror before him to saturate his mind. He moved from a deeper place within himself. He went to each person, shook and called out to them. In this way, he roused the least injured and helped them out of the bus unto the firm earth. They sat under the shade of a nearby tree like dazed sheep awaiting a shepherd. Meanwhile, Banny continued to work. Inside the coach he called, pulled and pried.

Those whom he could not awaken, he dislodged from their would-be coffins and half dragged, half carried them to the opening. Undaunted by the distance and angle of the upturned opening in relation to the ground, he devised a system of rolling each person up the make shift steps created by the folds in the door until they lay on the outer side of the bus. He then used the broken branches around the bus to facilitate a somewhat prickly but cushioned decent to the ground.

Once there, he pulled each person over to where the others sat. In this way, he extricated three women and four men. He could not tell if they were dead or alive.He would not allow himself to think about that. Finally, the only person left in the vehicle was Tapps whose left leg was pinned between the steering wheel and the driver's window. Banny sprang onto the tire and called again. He shook Tapps for all he was worth. "Wake up, Man!" He growled savagely at his friend slapping the right side of his face with his palm. "Your son is waiting to see you, man. Wake up!" With a final slap, Banny grabbed hold of Tapps' boney nose and pinched it shut. "Wake up!"

Suddenly, Tapps sputtered like an engine igniting after several attempts. He gasped for air and swore when he realized that Banny was the one denying him oxygen. Banny let go of his nose then commanded, "Let's go. We have to get these people to hospital!" He said it as if there was no obstacle and all Tapps had to do was get up. He was so convincing that Tapps instinctively tried to rouse himself. That was when the full measure of his situation became apparent and the memory of the crash flashed across his face. Banny did not share in his reverie. He was busily yanking at the steering wheel as if his own strength could dislodge it from its casing or, at the very least, bend it away from Tapps.

"There's an easier way." Tapps calmly touched Banny's hand and pointed to a lever on the steering column that adjusted the wheel. Banny flipped the lever. He was then able to move the wheel away from Tapps with ease. He helped Tapps out of the bus and they made it over to the crowd of tourists. Everyone was coming around. Miraculously, there had been no casualties. There appeared to be some broken limbs and several people were bleeding profusely but they were all alive. The shock was wearing off. Tears and fears were beginning to surface.

Banny again took command like a captain on a battlefield. "You are all hurt, we know that. We will get you to hospital as soon as possible. In the meantime, you must remain calm for your own safety. Fortunately for us, this area has mostly zebra and impala. You are safe here for now. Remember, wild animals can smell fear. They can also hear you very easily and sense when you have been injured. If you remain calm and stick together we will guarantee your safety." He said it so authoritatively no one dared challenge his statement.

The fact that they were in the middle of a long stretch of grassland with no sign of civilization temporarily escaped their consciousness. They were safe. Banny had just said it. He went back into the bus and located the overturned cooler of bottled water. He handed bottles to everyone and gave Tapps the first aid kit. "See what you can do. I'm going to get help." With that, he took off running.

Banny did not know where he was going. He ran at full clip, propelled by an inner force that did not explain itself. He found himself suddenly veering this way and that, speeding up and slowing down as the internal compass pointed the way. When he saw the small village of thatched huts, his pace quickened. As Banny approached the entrance, he slowed to a respectful walk. It was still early and the Zulu village was stirring as he entered the compound. A young woman tending a garden saw him first. He was still dressed in his tour guide attire but was drenched in sweat and barely able to speak. Her older brothers escorted him to the chief.

After a bowl of refreshing water, Banny was able to relate their predicament. The chief called for the Induna. He was an ancient man who moved slowly but he was sure-footed as an impala and his eyes held the glint of an eagle. He stood in his leopard skin apron and ornate headband looking at Banny without a word for a timeless moment. His piercing eyes asked and answered his questions as he took in the young man's appearance.

For his part, Banny withstood the appraisal with humility and patience. He knew that despite his sense of urgency, he had to respect the process and allow the holy man to make his pronouncement. And so it was.

Within a half-hour, the entire village had mobilized to help the stranded tour group. They brought ropes and animals. A few of them had old vehicles. They threaded the ropes through the windows of the bus and tied them to the vehicles and animals on one side while the young men and boys crowded along the other side of the bus.

It took several attempts but soon, the pulley system heaved the bus back unto its feet like a fallen rhinoceros finding his footing. Tapps, forgetting his injuries, jumped into the driver's seat and anxiously turned the key. The engine coughed and sputtered while everyone held their breath. But just as the sun reached the top branches of the acacia tree, the engine came to life.

The tribal women and children swarmed the inside of the bus with make shift brooms brushing away the broken glass from the seats and floor. There would be no air-conditioned comfort since all the windows had shattered when the vehicle overturned, but the bus was road worthy and ready to take them back to Cape Town. Once they were within range of cell phone towers, Banny called ahead and informed his office of their condition. The tour company had sent out a search party when the bus had not returned the evening before. But the numerous detours had resulted in an unsuccessful search.

The media was abuzz with the loss of forty-five foreigners in KwaZulu-Natal, the province of the Zulus. When the tour bus pulled into the station, there was a jumbled mixture of excitement and chaos. There were medics and ambulances present. The media was among the fray, exploiting the moment at every possible turn. Wind of Banny's bravery hit the streets through text messages and word of mouth even before it was breaking news on the local television stations. When it was discovered that he had suffered a dislocation of his right shoulder, the media went wild. "An amazing rescue!" said the Channel Six News. "Super-human strength!" Declared the tabloids. His tour company had immediately offered him a promotion. Two other companies had expressed interest in hiring him.

Banny was sitting up in the hospital bed with an immobilizing cast on his right shoulder and forearm. Never was seated on the bed beside him when a timid knock attracted their attention. They looked at each other quizzically. The media had treated his room like a thoroughfare over the past two days. It was not like them to be subtle. They weren't the only ones. Old acquaintances had shown up unannounced with bold professions of concern. People who had spurned him were crawling out of the wood work.

He got calls and texts from numbers he had previously deleted or just didn't recognize. Even his long estranged father had called to congratulate him. They seemed to all have conveniently forgotten that he was a gay man in a land where sexual orientation determined acceptance. Banny had handled all the attention with a great deal of equanimity. People had rejected him for being himself. He would not be moved by their fickle affections. The tentative knock sounded again.

"Come in!" Banny called. He swallowed hard when he saw his mother walk through the door. Never's hand went up to his mouth in shock. He immediately got up to leave the room. Banny reached out with his uninjured arm and grabbed his hand. "No", he said quietly. They waited silently as his mother made her way to his bed. She glanced at Never and nodded nervously.

Then, she looked into her son's eyes and spoke, "Banny, I heard the news. Saw you on television." She paused, uncharacteristically unsure of herself. "That was a really brave thing you did. I came here to say that..." Her voice trailed off; then she rushed on as if she was afraid she would lose her nerve and not complete her sentence. "I came here to say that despite everything," she glanced at Never as if he embodied the phrase, then she rushed on, "despite everything, you are still my son. We are still family and I am proud of you."

There was a long silence. Never squirmed. Ndosa stared blankly at a spot on the wall, waiting. She had surrendered enough of her pride by coming here. She turned to go. "The sun strengthened me." Ndosa stopped in mid stride. His words were echos of his return from his Abakhwetha so many years ago when she had feared she had lost her son. The memories rose up like the sun cresting the horizon and with it her emotions overflowed their banks. She had lost her son for a second time. She stood with her back to them, tears streaming down her face. "Mama." was all he said. And before they understood what was happening, she was sitting on the side of the bed cradling his head to her chest and they were both weeping.

Never stood beside them crying openly. Banny looked up at Never and tapped the free side of the bed. Never approached cautiously, then sat gingerly on the edge.

Ndosa looked up and he flinched like a skittish animal about to bolt. She looked into his eyes for the first time, ever. "I do not understand, I do not agree. But for the sake of love, I will accept."

He held her gaze and beyond the memories of harsh words and dark emotions, he could see the hint of a South African sunrise.

Lion's Head & Robben Island, Cape Town

Just Chasing the Sun

When I was young I ran after mother
Growing older I chased my child.

I chased after God and ran after love
But all I was doing was chasing the sun.

All I was doing was chasing the sun.

Up with the dawn to chase a dream
With its setting, still far from real
Chasing the dream which follows the earth,
Chasing the earth which follows the sun.

All I was doing was chasing the sun.

Some chase fame, some fortune and love,
Some want peace, some war, some sweet relief.
Whether war or peace, hate or love
All we are doing is chasing the sun.

All we are doing is chasing the sun.

Your schemes, my dreams, his fantasies
No more tangible, no more real.

Famine or feast, joy, sorrow or peace
We all seek that same ineffable release.

All we are doing is chasing the sun.

Ball of incandescence
Glowing brilliance filling the skies.

133

Just Chasing the Sun

Star of impermanence
Glorious splendor as it dies.

Yet all we are doing is chasing the sun.

Journey to nowhere, ego bound
Wretched and weary we seek to be found.

The rise and fall of each man's hope
Is this journey that chases the sun.

We are all just chasing the sun.

∞

Evolution

In the evolution of our minds
We have chosen the way of the Pharisees and Scribes;
More knowledge, more control, more of more.
… But the soul cries.

Time marks our path, power the ultimate quest.
The path a linear climb, no end in sight;
Sensing nonetheless a beginning, an end outside our grasp.
… As the soul dies.

Turning inward to our dying selves
Suddenly aware of the writhing withering soul
We throw it lines of knowledge, religious platitudes
… And still the soul cries.

Unable to reach it with our linear paths
We stand before the great divide;
Continue on the path of power or plunge
Into the fathomless Unknown?
… As the soul dies.

Some reach for another foothold
In their manmade mountain
Some let go and dive
Tumbling into the Cycle of Ultimate Truth
… And the soul sighs.

∞

135

Freed Slaves

They broke the chains only to enslave our minds.
We are confined within the stigmas,
The judgments, the limitations that we set.
We are slaves of divisions. Slaves of provision.
If we can't see it, we can't reach for it,
Can't even imagine it's there.
But we pretend to believe, afraid to face our doubts.
We live in fear.

And we call our fear Religion.
We conform without question
And try to believe what our hearts reject.
We stifle creativity and demand conformity.
So diversity finds new outlets; perversity it begets.

Freedom is brewing in the streets,
And it's dancing to a new beat.
It is wild and free and yet it's holy.

God gets the last laugh, turning our hypocrisies upside down.
He's going to the heart and He's breaking the chains,
He's tilling the soil once frozen.

A cold heart is not the way, His Spirit seems to say.
The way lies deep in the jungles of each heart.
This is the uncharted path.
Here are where the treasures of darkness lie.
Here I will find you and rescue you from yourself.
The devil has been defeated. You are your worst enemy,
He seems to say.
A freed slave is still a slave.
It's time for a new mentality;

A new identity.
One new man must emerge.
But unity is not found first in conformity, it's in diversity.
The judgments must fall.
Holiness is a higher call.

∞

The Sitting

Let me sit here forever
Gazing into the depths of eternity
Following the dark inviting paths of your gaze
Into the Secret Place where all is still.

Let me look at you
And you at me until we become one
In the stillness of the Now.

Let me see who you are
Indian Chieftess, African Queen
Tracing your history of wounded wisdom
That has birthed the patience of your soul.

Let me find that you do not end
But merge and become my beginning;
My portrait.

And when we part, as we must
Let me take with me the eternal stillness
Despite the turmoil's fury
Holding within my breast the beat of our oneness
Until we find our way back again
To this place of sweet repose,
For yet another sitting.

Benediction

Today, know that I have set aside this moment in time
To show you what has always been, will always be and what is yet
To be revealed as true:

I envelope you in My arms
And call you My Beloved
I heal your wounds and bless your life,
In joys and pains, with love.
I dance with you and sing to you
In the wind and the rain and the sun.

In the darkness of the night,
As you flee the fears of life
I am the ground on which you tread,
The light you hope to see.
And in your hopes for your tomorrows
In light, in darkness, in sunshine, in rain
I am the only Truth you seek.

As Here and Now,
Forevermore
I bless you
With My peace.

∞

Acknowledgements

I would like to acknowledge the friends who have, over the years, listened with open hearts to my poems and stories. My deepest gratitude to: Barrington Salmon, your affirmations of my work and your incredible patience never faltered; Michael Freeman, your belief in my abilities encouraged me to be bold; Lynette Ralph, your example as a consummate professional gave me an example to follow; and Sandra Goldson, who endured many endless poems in the name of friendship.

I am also grateful to all the churches that have invited me in to share, especially Faith, Hope & Love Ministries led by Pastors Karey and Judianna Freeman.

A special thanks to the members of the Tallahassee Authors Network (TAN), especially Mrs. Barbara Joe Williams. You all embodied the hope I carried and spurred me on to the completion of this work.

To my mother, who believes in me and to my daughters, "Natasha" and "Alexandria," who suffered through endless readings; you are the wind beneath my wings.

It goes without saying but I will say it nonetheless; this work would not be possible without the inspiration and guidance of the Friend and Lover who is the Lord of my life. To Him be the glory.

And finally, to **you**, the Reader:

I hope you have enjoyed, *Just Chasing the Sun: A unique collection of short stories and poems.*

Thank you for taking this journey with me. May you be blessed!

-DAB

2014

www.Dixieannblack.com

Made in the USA
Columbia, SC
18 January 2019